REAL ENGLISH WRITING THROUGH CORRECTIONS

ネイティブ添削で学ぶ英文ライティング

英語便
www.eigobin.com

研究社

Copyright © 2012 by Eigobin

REAL ENGLISH WRITING THROUGH CORRECTIONS

PRINTED IN JAPAN

まえがき
PREFACE

英文のメールやビジネスレターを書こうとする方は、まずは現在知っている単語や文法を使って、なんとか文書を作り上げようとするでしょう。そして経験を重ねて、新しく覚えた単語を使ってみる、辞書や文法書に掲載されている効果的な構文を採用してみる、違う言い方を考えてみるといったことを通して、さらに質の高い英文が書けるようになります。これが英文ライティング学習の基本ですし、どんな上級者の方も、おそらく日々こうした努力をつづけていることでしょう。

しかし、実際のビジネスシーンにおいては、あるいは学術論文を発表する際には、基本的に内容が明瞭で、かつ文法・語法的に正しい英文を書くことが求められます。海外の会社に英文メールで問い合わせてみたものの、こちらの意図したことがうまく伝わらなかった、あるいは自分の考えや意見を率直に伝える文書を発信してみたところ、予想に反して相手の気持ちを害してしまった、といった話を時どきうかがいます。

辞書や参考書の例文をそのまま引用しても状況にそぐわないことはよくあります。日本人的発想で英文を書いてしまい、相手に理解してもらえなかった、不自然に思われてしまった、という経験をお持ちの方もいると思います。私たちと異なる文化背景を持つ英米人に問題なく理解してもらえる英文を書くのは、いつの時代も大変むずかしいことです。

そこで、自分が書いた英文を「ネイティブスピーカーにチェックしてもらう」必要性が生じます。

しかし、一口に「ネイティブ・チェック」と言っても、「信用できるネ

イティブに見てもらう」ことが基本として求められます。実際に仕事で日々英語を書いている、英米文化・社会事情に関してバランスの取れた知識を有している、外国人に英文ライティングを指導した経験があるなど、英文チェックのできるネイティブスピーカーには、やはりいくつか条件があります。

　さらに、プロのネイティブ・チェッカーに校閲を依頼するとなると、それなりのお金がかかってしまいます。この問題も、日本人英語学習者の大きな障害になっていると思われます。

　私たち「英語便」は、そんな日本人英語学習者と使用者の気持ちにお応えしたいと思い、2005年にサービスを開始しました。以来、多くのご利用者に支えられ、おかげさまで2012年に7年目を迎えました。2011年12月現在、累計メンバー数は1万人以上、継続メンバー数は2000人以上です。

　また、「お手頃な値段でネイティブ添削を提供する」こともサービス・ミッションの1つとしており、6ヶ月で1万9800円のコースからご用意しています（2012年1月現在）。

　英語便の講師は、もちろん全員が英語を母語とするネイティブスピーカーです。アメリカ人をはじめとして、カナダ人、イギリス人、オーストラリア人、ニュージーランド人ほかのメンバーを集めています。全員がプロのライターやジャーナリストであり、ほかにも大手企業のビジネス英語クラスの講師や英検二次試験の面接委員など、各方面の英文ライティングのスペシャリストを10人そろえています。

　英語便のネイティブ添削は、特に「自然な語感を伝える」ことに焦点を置いています。メンバー1人ひとりから提出される1つひとつの英文記事を、10人のネイティブスピーカーが念入りに確認して、必要に応じて修正を施し、さらには明瞭で具体的な解説や用例も付けて、基本的に

24時間以内、遅くとも48時間以内にお返ししています。
　たとえTOEIC900点以上のスコアを持っている方でも、ネイティブスピーカーから見ると、不自然な英語を書いていることも少なくありません。当サービスの2011年度の提出英文傾向分析では、文章全体の10%以上が不明瞭または不自然と判断される英文を書いたメンバー数が、全メンバー数の2割を超えています（TOEIC 900点以上の英語便のメンバーのなかから100人をランダムに抽出し、2011年1月から6月までの6ヶ月間において調査した結果です）。「英語便」は、このように上級者の方たちの英文ライティングの添削も受け付けています。
　また、これまで英語便で添削を受け付けた1万人以上の方たちの英文ライティング傾向を分析し、日本人英語学習者がよく間違える英語の使い方と、その修正ポイントをデータに蓄積し、サイトで公開しています。さらに「コミュニティ」では、メンバー間で英語の使い方に関する議論が毎日活発に行なわれています。その情報も随時データに反映しています。
　以上、詳しくは、実際に英語便のサイト（www.eigobin.com）を確認してみてください。

　本書『ネイティブ添削で学ぶ英文ライティング』は、ここでご紹介した英語便の様々なオンライン学習コンテンツを盛り込んだ紙媒体での初の公式学習ツールです。英語便がこれまで蓄積してきた学習ノウハウをもとに、日本人英語学習者がなかなか気づかないネイティブ視点による英文ライティングの書き方を、紙幅が許す限り、情報として盛り込みました。
　本書では、実際に英語便のメンバーが書いて提出し、ネイティブ講師がていねいに添削し、解説を付けたものを、重要例文とあわせて、でき

る限り紹介しました。実際の英語便ではネイティブ講師は添削の解説を英語で行なっていますが、ここでは英語の解説に慣れていない方にもネイティブ添削の面白さと有効性を理解していただくために、それをすべて日本語で付けました。

　英文添削例も、ビジネスメール8本、ビジネス文書6本、プライベートメール6本、ショートエッセイ1本のほか、TOEFL iBT, 英検1級、TOEIC SW テストのライティング問題も収録しました。読者のみなさまには、それぞれ目的に応じた英文の書き方を学んでいただきたいと思います。

　また、本書を読み終えた読者のみなさまに実際にネイティブ添削を体験していただきたいと考えて、英語便のサイトでは「無料添削サービス」もご用意しました（詳しくは211ページをご覧ください）。ぜひこちらもチャレンジしてみてください。みなさまのご応募をお待ちしております。

　本書を通じて、読者のみなさまが、自然な英語感覚を身に付けて、ネイティブ顔負けの英語が書けるようになっていただけますことを、英語便のスタッフ一同、願ってやみません。

　本書出版にあたり、課題の添削例の掲載にご協力いただいた英語便のメンバーのみなさま、そして貴重なご意見をお寄せくださったすべての方に、心より感謝申し上げます。

　また、末筆ながら、研究社編集部の金子靖さんには、企画から構成まで、一方ならぬお世話になりました（実は金子さんも英語便の熱心なメンバーの1人なのです）。この場を借りて、金子さんに厚くお礼申し上げます。

　2012年1月7日

英語便　スタッフ一同

目次 CONTENTS

まえがき　PREFACE ... iii

✉ I. 基礎編　BASIC COURSE　　1

1. 不適切な接続詞 ... 3
2. 不要なカンマ ... 4
3. 自信のない意見 ... 5
4. 単数 or 複数 ... 7
5. 多用される構文　not only A but also B ... 8
6. 多用される構文　neither A nor B ... 10
7. 間接表現 It 〜 for 〜 to 〜 ... 11
8. 不釣合いな修飾 ... 13

✎ II. ネイティブ添削実践編　PRACTICAL COURSE　　15

ビジネスメール①　自己紹介 ... 17
ビジネスメール②　商品の問い合わせ ... 24
ビジネスメール③　アポを取る ... 32
ビジネスメール④　お詫び ... 41
ビジネスメール⑤　注文を出す ... 50
ビジネスメール⑥　金額を交渉する ... 57
ビジネスメール⑦　招待する ... 66
ビジネスメール⑧　クレーム ... 74

ビジネス文書① 年頭の挨拶と商品について	83
ビジネス文書② 新製品の発表	91
ビジネス文書③ 開催延期のお知らせ	97
ビジネス文書④ 英文履歴書	103
ビジネス文書⑤ 操作マニュアル	111
ビジネス文書⑥ ミーティングのお知らせ	117
プライベートメール① プレゼントのお礼	123
プライベートメール② 誕生日のお祝い	130
プライベートメール③ 旅行に誘う	137
プライベートメール④ 誘いを断る	146
プライベートメール⑤ 感動を伝える	152
プライベートメール⑥ 友人を励ます	160
ショートエッセイ 問題点をまとめる	167
各種英文ライティング試験① TOEFL iBT®	173
各種英文ライティング試験② 英検1級	185
各種英文ライティング試験③ TOEIC SW® テスト	196

III. 英語便添削チャレンジ編 CHALLENGING COURSE 209

［課題1］ビジネスメール	212
［課題2］プライベートメール	214
［課題3］ショートエッセイ	216

重要英語表現索引　218

I.
基礎編
BASIC COURSE

基礎編では、「英文ライティングの思わぬ落とし穴」について、説明しています。外国人とメールなどの文書のやりとりに慣れていない方は、学校で習った正しいはずの文章が、なぜネイティブスピーカーには不自然に思えてしまうのか、よく理解できないことがあります。英語便の受講者（メンバー）のなかにも、添削結果を見て、自分のライティングのどこがおかしいのか、はっきり認識できない人もいます。

　ここでは、ネイティブスピーカーの添削を見たときに日本人学習者が困惑しやすい点について、実際に英語便のメンバーの人たちから寄せられたよくある質問を元に8項目を挙げて説明しています。ネイティブ添削実践編を読みはじめる前に、まずこの基礎編に目を通してください。今まで習ってきた英語の落とし穴に気づき、英文ライティングの面白さが理解いただけると思います。本編でネイティブスピーカーの添削の感じをつかんでいただくことで、次のネイティブ添削実践編の理解も深まると期待しております。

1. 不適切な接続詞

✏️ 提出者の英文例
I heard the drum or the whistle at the festival.

✍️ ネイティブの添削
I heard the drum and the whistle at the festival.

✉️ 提出者の反応
太鼓と笛を両方一緒に聞いたわけではないので、意味が違うと思います。

👉 解説
「お祭りで太鼓や笛の音を聞いた」と日本語で考えて書かれた文です。
「〜と〜」は and,「〜または〜」は or という理解は一般的には正しいのですが、日本語と英語の考え方は異なります。and と or のあいだの意味の境界線と、「〜と〜」と「〜または〜」のあいだの意味の境界線とでは、若干ずれがあります。例文のように、日本語では「〜や〜」と表現するのが適当で、「時どき起こるもの、また散らばっているもの」を表わすときは、英語では and を使うのが適切です。しかし、この場合に日本人学習者は or を使ってしまうことがよくあるようです。

例文のように太鼓や笛があちこちでばらばらに聞こえるような場面では、通常 and を使います。or を使うと「太鼓または笛の音を聞いた」という語感がおかしな文になってしまいます。

▼ 追加添削例

John likes playing the guitar or watching movies.
⇨ **John likes playing the guitar and watching movies.**

2. 不要なカンマ

✏️ 提出者の英文例
I liked that movie, too.

✍️ ネイティブの添削
I liked that movie too.

✉️ 提出者の反応
too の前にはカンマを入れると学校で学びました。この添削はほんとうに正しいのですか？

👉 解説
実際には、too の前にカンマはあってもなくてもかまいません。ただし、カンマのあるときと、ないときでは、文のニュアンスが異なります。

I liked that movie, too. とカンマのある文では、too の前のカンマで読み手が一拍を置くことで、「私も」の「も」の部分を強調するセンテンスになります。

単に「私もその映画が気に入りました」という意味を伝えたいときは、通常 I liked that movie too. のように、カンマを使わずに表現します。

日本人英語学習者の提出英文を見ていると、副詞や副詞句の前後に必要ないと思われるカンマを時どき打ってしまっていることがよくあります。カンマの場所をルールで覚えるだけではなく、カンマを使うことで文のニュアンスが変わってしまうことを理解し、よく考えて使う必要があります。

> ▼ 追加添削例
>
> I, too, like that movie.
> ⇨ **I too like that movie.**
>
> I haven't gotten to my studying, yet.
> ⇨ **I haven't gotten to my studying yet.**
>
> Last summer, I went to France on business.
> ⇨ **Last summer I went to France on business.**

　以下のような副詞を文頭で使うときは、そのあとに通常カンマを打ちます。カンマを入れることで、文の流れの変化を明確に伝えるためです。

Also,
Therefore,
However,
Moreover,
Furthermore,

3. 自信のない意見

✏️ 提出者の英文例
I think a new energy policy could effect the economy.

🖍 ネイティブの添削
I think a new energy policy will effect the economy.

✉️ 提出者の反応
「新しいエネルギー政策が経済効果をもたらすかもしれない」という考え方

について、could を使って仮定的な表現にしたかったのです。will ではセンテンスの意味が変わってしまいます。

👉 解説

「新しいエネルギー政策が経済効果をもたらすかもしれないと考える」というセンテンスは、日本語では問題ないように見えます。ところが、I think でセンテンスをはじめることで、「これは自分の考えであり、事実を述べているわけではない」と読み手に伝わってしまいます。

英文では、自分の考えに、may や could などの仮定・推量の助動詞を使うと、せっかく書いた考えに自信がないように響いてしまいます。また仮定・推量を表わす助動詞を多用することで、「書き手は内容について確信がないまま文を書いている」と読み手に悪い印象を与えることもあります。

「〜かもしれない」「〜であろう」は、日本語では考え方を伝える表現として、日常的に使われます。しかし、それをそのまま英語の may や could で表現しようとすると、ニュアンスが変わってしまいます。普通に自分の意見を表明したいときは、「〜かもしれない」「〜であろう」という日本語の間接表現を英語の may や could に当てはめるのではなく、可能な限り直接的に表現して、自分の意見を明確に伝え、より英語らしい表現にすることを心がけましょう。

Eigobin Pointers may, could などの仮定・推量の助動詞の代わりに will を使うことで、より直接的な表現となります。

▼ 追加添削例

Solar energy may become a major source of energy.
⇨ **Solar energy will become a major source of energy.**

4. 単数 or 複数

✏️ 提出者の英文例
I have fruits for breakfast.

✍️ ネイティブの添削
I have **fruit** for breakfast.

✉️ 提出者の反応
「朝食にフルーツを食べる」と言いたかったのです。通常、1個ではなく、いくつか食べるので、fruit は fruits と複数形にすべきではないでしょうか？

👉 解説
単語 fruit は、可算名詞／不可算名詞の両方のフォームがあり、「フルーツ」という総称を表わす場合は不可算名詞 fruit を用います。例文のように、「朝食に（何らかの）フルーツを食べる」というような、特に種類を特定しない場合は、この総称としての不可算名詞 fruit を使います。

一方、特定のフルーツ数種を頭のなかに浮かべることができる場合は、以下のように複数形を使うことができます。下の例文では、特定のいくつかのフルーツ種（たとえば、マンゴー、パパイヤなどのトロピカルフルーツ）にアレルギーがあるという意味を表わします。

[例] I'm allergic to some **fruits**.

Eigobin Pointers 上の複数形の利用例は、おもにアメリカ英語で使われます。イギリス英語では、複数種を表わす場合、不可算名詞をそのまま使い、I'm allergic to some kinds of fruit. のように表現します。

> ▼ 追加添削例
> Are you ready to order some foods?
> ⇨ Are you ready to order some **food**?

Eigobin Pointers　単語 food も、fruit 同様、「食べ物」という概念を表わすときは、不可算名詞 food を使います。

5. 多用される構文　not only A but also B

✏️ 提出者の英文例
Yesterday my wife went not only to Shinjuku but also Shibuya.

🖊 ネイティブの添削
Yesterday my wife went to Shinjuku, then Shibuya.

✉️ 提出者の反応
どうして修正されたのか、よくわかりません。

👉 解説
　Yesterday my wife went not only to Shinjuku but also Shibuya. という英文は、「私の妻は新宿だけではなく、渋谷にも行った」と考えて書かれた文だと思います。文法的には何の問題もないのですが、ネイティブスピーカーがこのセンテンスを見ると、苦笑してしまいます。

　not only A but also B の構文は、文を組み立てやすいので、日本人英語学習者があらゆる場面で使う傾向があります。この構文は「A だけでなく B も」「A のみならず B も」という意味ですが、実際には A と B をあえて対比する場面で使われるため、not only A「〜のみならず」の A の部分は、

「現状」「周知の事実」または「一般常識」、but also B の B の部分は、「新しい事実」や「実はこうなんですという驚き」として書かれるのが一般的です。

以下、例文で解説します。

[例1]　**Eat not only meat but also vegetables.**
　　　　肉ばかり食べていないで、野菜を食べなさい。

A の部分の周知の事実と B の部分でこれからの新しいことを対比しています。英文として問題ありません。

[例2]　**She is not only beautiful but also kind to everyone.**
　　　　彼女は美しいだけでなく、みんなに親切だ。

A の彼女は美しいという部分と、B のみんなに親切だという驚き（美人は冷たいという印象に反して親切である）を対比しています。これも英文として、問題ありません。

では、もう一度、オリジナルの提出者の文を見てみます。

Yesterday my wife went not only to Shinjuku but also Shibuya.

書いている夫にとっては、妻が渋谷にも行ったことが驚きだった可能性もありますが、読み手にとっては、新宿が先でも渋谷が先でも、どちらでもいい話です。
このように、A と B の対比がそれほど強調すべきことでないにもかかわらず、not only A but also B 構文を使ってしまうと、なんだかおおげさに聞こえてしまうことがあり、時に苦笑されてしまったりするので、注意しましょう。

> ▼ 追加添削例
> I like not only action movies but also science fiction movies.
> ⇨ **I like both action and science fiction movies.**

6. 多用される構文　neither A nor B

🖉 提出者の英文例
I like neither mustard nor ketchup.

✍ ネイティブの添削
I don't like mustard or ketchup.

✉ 提出者の反応
オリジナルの文と、どこが違うのでしょうか？

☞ 解説

　実は、I like neither mustard nor ketchup. という文には何も悪いところはなく、意味も問題なく通じます。

　どうやら一般の日本人英語学習者は、(1) both A and B（AとBの両方）、(2) either A or B（AまたはBのどちらか）、(3) neither A nor B（AとBのどちらでもない）という3つのパターンを学校で習うためか、2つの事象を書き表わそうとするときに、いずれかのパターンに当てはめて文を作ろうとする傾向があるようです。そのため、例文にあるような neither A nor B という構文を必要以上に使う人が多いように思います。

　一方、ネイティブスピーカーが、実際 neither A nor B を使う場面は多くないのです。「日本の学校で文法を教える以外は、1回も使ったことがない」という人も少なくありません。

neither A nor B という構文を使ってはいけないということではないし、それが不自然であるということもないのですが、日常あまり見ないことから、ネイティブスピーカーが「私ならこう言う」という視点で文を直すと、別の言い方に直されることがよくあります。

▼ 追加添削例
Most vegetarians eat neither meat nor fish.
⇨ **Most vegetarians don't eat meat or fish.**

7. 間接表現 It ～ for ～ to ～

📝 提出者の英文例
It's not easy for me to learn foreign languages.

✍️ ネイティブの添削
Learning foreign languages is not easy for me.

✉️ 提出者の反応
構文の違いはわかるのですが、提出文のどこが悪いのでしょうか？

👉 解説
It's not easy for me to learn foreign languages. という文は、英語として完璧です。ただ、「外国語を学ぶのは簡単ではない」と言いたいときは、ネイティブ添削例にあるように、Learning foreign languages is not easy for me. と直接的な言い方をしたほうがいいように思います。It's not easy for me to learn foreign languages. は、先行代名詞 it を文頭に出した間接表現であり、この場合はややふさわしくないように思えます。It is ～で書きはじめる構文では、「～することは～である」の「～である」の部

分に、より重点が置かれます。したがって、「簡単ではない」という部分が強調されてしまうのです。これに対して、Learning foreign languages is not easy for me. は、「外国語を学ぶことは」という内容をまず読み手が考えます。

　文が組み立てやすいためか、日本人英語学習者のなかには、「〜することは〜である」と聞くと、It is 〜とすぐに書きはじめる人も少なくありません。しかし、注意してほしいのは、この構文はセンテンスを最後まで読まないと主語が何であるのかわからないので、時に読み手にあいまいな印象を与えてしまうということです。

　英語で文を書くときは、「直接的に表わせる場面では、直接的な表現にする」、また、「意味やスタイルを考えて、必要に応じて適切な構文を用いる」ことを心がけましょう。

　It is 〜で書きはじめる構文の使い方としては、以下の例のように、主語の「〜することは」の部分が長い文に関しては、代名詞 it を文頭に出せば、読みやすくすることができます。

［例1］　主語が長くて読みにくい文
Learning foreign languages by just speaking with people from abroad is not easy for me.

［例2］　it を文頭に置いて、読みやすくした文
It's not easy for me to learn foreign languages by just speaking with people from abroad.

▼ 追加添削例
It's fun to play tennis.
⇨ **Playing tennis is fun.**

8. 不釣合いな修飾

✏️ 提出者の英文例
I was very terrified.

✍️ ネイティブの添削
I was terrified.

✉️ 提出者の反応
強調の意味で very を使ったのですが、間違いなのでしょうか？

👉 解説
　副詞の very（とても）は、後続の形容詞を強調する際に使いますが、terrified（おびえた）という形容詞は、very で強調するまでもなく、絶対的に強い意味を持っています。こういった形容詞は non-gradable adjectives（程度が変えられない形容詞）と見なされ、通常は単体で I was terrified. のように使われます。

　ただし、very は使えなくても、terrified のような non-gradable adjectives を修飾できる副詞があります。こうした副詞は、non-gradable adverbs（程度が変えられない副詞）と呼ばれます。

　non-gradable adverbs は、絶対的な形容詞の意味をさらに強調することができます。

　以下に、non-gradable adverbs と non-gradable adjectives の組み合わせ例を示します。

non-gradable adverbs	non-gradable adjectives
absolutely	awful
utterly	excellent
completely	terrified
totally	impossible

一方、very のような副詞は、gradable adverbs（程度が変えられる副詞）と呼ばれ、副詞によって程度が変化する形容詞（gradable adjectives）とペアで使うことができます。

gradable adverbs	gradable adjectives
a little	angry
very	hot
slightly	important
extremely	rich

　副詞＋形容詞については、これらの基本的な組み合わせルールについて押さえておくことで、効果的な文を書くことができます。

Eigobin Pointers　ただし、It's a fairly impossible job. のように、例外で組み合わせを変えることができる副詞と形容詞のペアもあるので、注意が必要です。

▼ 追加添削例

The movie was very awful.
⇨ **The movie was absolutely awful.**

II. ネイティブ添削 実践編
PRACTICAL COURSE

ネイティブ添削実践編では、ビジネスメール、ビジネス文書、プライベートメール、ショートエッセイ、各種英文ライティング試験の5分野において、英語便の受講者（メンバー）が実際に書いた英文に対して、ネイティブスピーカーの講師が詳細な添削・解説を行なっています。

　英文法の細かい解説だけでなく、読みやすくする文章作法、冠詞・前置詞のニュアンスの違い、また海外への発信時に注意すべきことなど、ライティングに関するあらゆる留意事項について、詳しく触れています。文法ルールを確認するだけでなく、文章のトーンや細かい英語のニュアンスも意識しながら、読み進めてください。英語の感覚が養われ、各英語表現のニュアンスがつかめるようになると、自然で洗練された英文を書くことができるようになります。

　また、各ライティング例の最後に、同テーマで講師が書き下ろした英文が掲載されています。添削を反映した受講者の英文ライティング文書と、ネイティブスピーカーが書き下ろした文書ではいったいどこが違うのか、よく確認してみてください。

✉ ビジネスメール ①

自己紹介

[メンバー情報]
田中　理恵様／営業職／29歳

[文の説明]
新しい役職に就いたことを、取引先の関係者へ知らせるメールです。

✏ 原文

01. Dear Mr. Smith,

02. I'm Rie Tanaka at ABC Co. Ltd. I am writing this email to you because I was referred to you by Mr. Teruo Kamoda.

03. I have become a manager of Pan Pacific division since spring, and will also be in charge of the next World Expo.

04. I heard you were working in so many International exhibition projects. I would like to hear about your opinions about our next event near future.

05. Please drop in and see me when you happen to come this way.

06. Yours sincerely,

07. Rie Tanaka

✍️ 添削

01. Dear Mr. Smith,

02. I'm Rie Tanaka at ABC Co. Ltd. I am writing this email to you because I was referred to you by Mr. Teruo Kamoda.

03. I have ~~become~~ been a manager of the Pan Pacific division since spring, and will also be in charge of the next World Expo.

04. I heard you were working ~~in~~ on so many international exhibition projects. I would like to hear ~~about~~ your opinions about our next event in the near future.

05. Please drop in and see me ~~when you happen to come this way~~ when you are in Japan.

06. Yours sincerely,

07. Rie Tanaka

👉 解説

03 過去のある時点から現在まで、あるポジションに就いているという場合、have been（以前から～である）という表現を用います。
　例を挙げて説明します。

[例1] **I've been the organizer** of this group since it started in

June 2011.
私は、2011年の6月から、このグループのまとめ役を務めています。

また、「過去に仕事で昇進した」という意味であれば、have become ではなく、got promoted, was (were) promoted が一般的に使われます。got promoted と was (were) promoted のあいだに意味やニュアンスの違いはありません。以下、それぞれの例を挙げて説明します。

［例2］ **I got promoted to the position of senior clerk.**
私は上級職員に昇進した。

［例3］ **I was promoted to the position of assistant supervisor.**
私はアシスタントスーパーバイザーへ昇進した。

Eigobin Pointers senior clerk, assistant supervisor などの役職を、一般総称として使うときは、position of ～（～の地位）を追加します。一方、社内固有の役職名として使うときは、Senior Clerk, Assistant Supervisor のように頭を大文字にして、そのままにします。
以下、例を示します。

［例4］ **I got promoted to Senior Clerk.**
［例5］ **I was promoted to Assistant Supervisor.**

Eigobin Pointers a manager of the Pan Pacific division と、不定冠詞 a を使って表現すると、複数の manager のうちの1人であることを意味します。1人の manager が部署全体を管理している場合は、the manager of the Pan Pacific division と定冠詞 the を使うべきです。

04 「プロジェクトに取り組む」と言うときに、work につづく前置詞は in ではなく on を使います。
以下、work on を使った例を挙げて説明します。

[例1]　**I am now working on a big project.**
　　　　私は今大きなプロジェクトに取り組んでいる。

Eigobin Pointers　本文中の you were working on so many international exhibition projects という表現は、スミスさんがたくさんのプロジェクトで働いていたという過去の出来事を意味します。

　もし、スミスさんが過去からたくさんのプロジェクトで働いてきており、今もそのフィールドにいる（今後もつづけていくであろうと予想される）場合は、以下のように現在完了を使うべきです。

[例2]　**I've heard you have worked on so many international exhibition projects.**

　「意見を聞く」と言う場合、hear のあとに、前置詞の about は不要です。in the near future は、「近いうちに」という意味の定型句です。

05　happen to come this way は、「こちらにおいでの際は」という日本語表現には近いですが、ネイティブスピーカーには少々まわりくどく聞こえます。
　以下のように具体的に書くことで、英語らしい表現になります。

[例]　**Please drop in and see me when you are in Tokyo.**

06　日本語の「敬具」などにあたる結びの言葉（complimentary close）は、ビジネスで取引先にあてるような改まった場合は、Sincerely yours または Yours sincerely がいちばん無難です。親しい間柄であれば、Yours がよく使われます。また、regards（尊敬、敬意）を使って、Best regards あるいは（With）kind [kindest] regards や（With）warm [warmest] regards という言い方もよくされます。

添削反映バージョン

Dear Mr. Smith,

I'm Rie Tanaka at ABC Co. Ltd. I am writing this email to you because I was referred to you by Mr. Teruo Kamoda.

I have been a manager of the Pan Pacific division since spring, and will also be in charge of the next World Expo.

I heard you were working on so many international exhibition projects.

I would like to hear your opinions about our next event in the near future.

Please drop in and see me when you are in Japan.

Yours sincerely,

Rie Tanaka

同テーマで講師が書き下ろしたバージョン

Dear Mr. Smith,

My name is Rie Tanaka and I am a manager at the Pan Pacific division of ABC Co. Ltd. Mr. Teruo Kamoda, who works with me, recommended that I write to you as I will be in charge of the next World Expo.

Mr. Kamoda mentioned that you have worked on many projects for the international exhibits and I would like to get your views about our next event. Please let me know when you will be in Japan next so that we can set up a meeting to discuss the event. If you will not be visiting Japan in the near future, perhaps we can set up a conference call.

I look forward to hearing from you.

Regards,

Rie Tanaka

「同テーマで講師が書き下ろしたバージョン」語注

□ **exhibit**（名詞）「展示会」
　名詞の exhibit は「出品物、展示物」という意味もあります。exhibit はアメリカ英語では「展示会」という意味でよく使われます。イギリス英語では、

exhibit は展示物を指すことが多く、「展示会」の意味では exhibition のほうがよく使われます。

[例] **The Picasso exhibit is here until the end of the month.**
ピカソの展示会は月末までここで行なわれている。

□ **view**（名詞）「意見、見解」

get one's view で、「～の意見（見解）を得る」という意味になります。

[例] **I don't get his view on global warming.**
地球温暖化についての彼の見解は理解できない。

□ **conference call**（名詞）「電話会議」

[例] **It's hard to arrange conference calls because of the time difference.**
時差があるので、電話会議を手配するのは大変だ。

✉ ビジネスメール ②

商品の問い合わせ

[メンバー情報]
M.S. 様／その他／44 歳

[文の説明]
海外の化粧品メーカーが作っているハンドクリームを、独自の容器に入れて商品化し、輸入する手配を進めるメールです。

 原文

---

01. Dear Mr. Anderson,

02. Thank you for sending your samples of hand cream.

03. They are very comfortable to use and we are considering importing of non perfume one first.

04. We would like to put it in a round plastic container. We are searching high quality and reasonably priced containers here but we cannot find any so far. If you know any good manufacturers, please let us know about them. We think that 50g is a good size for the new product.(The diameter would be 5-6cm.)

05. The F.O.B. price of this product should be under US$2.00, including the container.

06. In addition, we need detailed ingredients which The Pharmaceutical Law in Japan requires us.

07. It would be very helpful to us if you send it by email as soon as possible.

08. Thank you for your kind cooperation.

09. Best Regards,

10. Michiko Saijo

 添削

01. Dear Mr. Anderson,

02. Thank you for sending your hand cream samples ~~of hand cream~~.

03. They are very ~~comfortable~~ luxurious ~~to use~~ and we are considering importing ~~of the~~ ~~non perfume~~ unscented one first.

04. We would like to put it in a round plastic container. We are searching for high quality and reasonably priced containers here but we ~~cannot find~~ haven't found any so far. If you know any good manufacturers, please let us know about them. We think that 50g is a good size for the new product.

(The diameter ~~would~~ should be 5-6cm.)

05. The F.O.B. price of this product should be under US$2.00, including the container.

06. In addition, we need a detailed ~~ingredients~~ ingredient list which ~~The Pharmaceutical Law~~ pharmaceutical laws in Japan requires ~~us~~.

07. It would be very helpful to us if you could send it by email as soon as possible.

08. Thank you for your kind cooperation.

09. Best Regards,

10. Michiko Saijo

👉 解説

02 samples of hand cream は、hand cream samples とするほうが簡潔です。

Eigobin Pointers hand cream samples のように2つ以上の名詞が合わさって1つの名詞となるものを複合名詞といいます。

日本語の「〜の」という表現をそのまま of に置き換えると、冗長な表現になりがちです。適切な複合名詞を使うと、すっきりした表現になります。以下、例を示します。

［例1］ **a test of English grammar** ⇨ **an English grammar test**

[例2]　**a teacher of math**　⇨　**a math teacher**

03　ここでは、単語 comfortable を、「使い勝手がいい」といった意味で使っているのだと思いますが、comfortable はおもに心や体の状態を言い表わすときに使う形容詞であり、ハンドクリームのよさを表現する用語としては不適切です。
　以下、ハンドクリームに使えるいくつかの形容詞を例示します。

[例]
luxurious（贅沢な）
soothing（心地よい）
smooth（滑らかな）
nice（素敵な）

　~ to use の to use の部分は、文脈から読み取れるので冗長に聞こえます。ここでは不要です。
　「無香料の」という形容詞は non-perfumed と表わせます。ただし、unscented のほうがより一般的に使われています。
　「~を輸入すること」は、importing ~と表わせるため、of は不要です。
　メールの相手は、そのプロダクトについてすでに認識があるため、ここでは the unscented one と定冠詞 the を使うのが適切です。

04　「~を探す」は search for ~と前置詞 for が必要です。
Eigobin Pointers　searching for を使うと、「既存の容器のなかから探している」という意味になります。「調査中」と言う場合は、researching を使うのが適切です。
　we cannot find ~ という表現は、すでに探すことをやめてしまったように聞こえます。ここでは、we haven't found ~として、「まだちょうどよい容器は見つかっていないが、引き続き探している」という意味を出すのが適切です。
Eigobin Pointers　I haven't found any のような否定の現在完了の文は、過去か

ら現在までに何かができていない状態を表わしていますが、未来にはなされるであろうことを暗示しています。
以下、例を挙げて説明します。

［例］ **I haven't checked** my email this week.
今週はメールをチェックしていない。（⇨ そのうちチェックするつもりだ）

The diameter would be 5-6cm は、「直径は5～6センチだろうと思う」とあいまいな表現になるため、should を使って「～すべきです」とするのが適切です。

06 need detailed ingredients は、あたかも実際にオフィスに原材料を送るかのような印象を与えてしまいます。ここでは「原材料のリスト」のことを言っているので、a detailed ingredient list とするのがいいでしょう。

また、The Pharmaceutical Law のように、大文字で法律名を書くと、実際の正式な法律名と受け取られてしまいます。ここでは包括的な意味での法律を指していると思われますので pharmaceutical laws と小文字、そして複数形にするのがいいと思います。複数形にすることで、「薬事法」のみならず、関連法令など全般を指すことができます。

主語が law → laws と複数形になるため、requires を require にします。

日本の法律は日本国民全体 (us) が名宛人になっているため、require us の us は省略できます。

修正された文 a detailed ingredient list which pharmaceutical laws in Japan require でも意味は通じますが、以下のように文体を変えることで、よりフォーマルで自然な英文になります。

［例1］ **a detailed ingredient list as required by the pharmaceutical laws in Japan**

［例2］ **a detailed ingredient list which is required under Japanese law**

07 you could send のように could を使い、間接的な文にすることで、よりていねいでやわらかい言い方になります。

> 添削反映バージョン

Dear Mr. Anderson,

Thank you for sending your hand cream samples.

They are very luxurious and we are considering importing the unscented one first.

We would like to put it in a round plastic container. We are searching for high quality and reasonably priced containers here but we haven't found any so far. If you know any good manufacturers, please let us know about them.

We think that 50g is a good size for the new product. (The diameter should be 5-6cm.)

The F.O.B. price of this product should be under US$2.00, including the container.

In addition, we need a detailed ingredient list as required by the pharmaceutical laws in Japan. It would be very helpful to us if you could send it by email as soon as possible.

Thank you for your kind cooperation.

Best Regards,

Michiko Saijo

同テーマで講師が書き下ろしたバージョン

Dear Mr. Anderson,

Thank you for sending us the hand cream samples. Overall, we were impressed with the quality and texture of them and would like to import the unscented one on a trial basis.

Ideally, we would like to package it in round, plastic 50 gram containers that are about 5-6cm in diameter. Unfortunately, we have been unable to find a container that would work so if you could introduce us to any packaging or container manufacturers it would be greatly appreciated. As a guideline, the F.O.B. price of the product, including the container, is under $2.00 so a manufacturer that could work within that guideline is best.

In addition, pharmaceutical laws in Japan require a detailed list of ingredients. We would appreciate it if you could send us this information as soon as possible.

Thank you again for the samples and we look forward to working with you on this project.

Regards,

Michiko Saijo

「同テーマで講師が書き下ろしたバージョン」語注

□ **overall** （副詞）「全体的に」
　［例］　**Overall things have improved.**
　　　　全体的に物事は好転している。
「全体的に」という意味では、for the most part, all in all, by and large といった表現もあります。

□ **on a trial basis**「試験的に」
　［例］　**He has been hired on a trial basis for three months.**
　　　　彼は試験的に3ヶ月間雇われた。

□ **it would be greatly appreciated**「大変助かります」
　［例1］　**If anyone has a solution to this problem it would be greatly appreciated.**
　　　　もしどなたかがこの問題の解決方法をご存知でしたら、大変助かります。
it would be greatly appreciated はかなりフォーマルな表現です。もう少しだけた場面で、「大変助かります」「幸いです」と言いたい場合は、I would really appreciate it if 〜 という表現がよく使われます。
　［例2］　**I would really appreciate it if you finish it by the end of the day.**
　　　　もし今日中に終わらせていただけますと、大変助かります。

✉ ビジネスメール ③

アポを取る

[メンバー情報]
斉藤　新様／ビジネスコンサルタント／34歳

[文の説明]
　ビデオカンファレンスでしか面識のないアメリカの取引先の担当者に、訪問のアポ（アポイントメント）を取るメールです。

✎ 原文

01. Hello Mr. Watson,

02. I'm Shin Saito. I am emailing because I will be visiting Washington next month to attend the JDEX Expo, and I would like to drop by your company and introduce myself if you are available.

03. I will be in the U.S. from September 2nd to 8th, and I will be free after the expo on the 4th.

04. If you are available, I would like to visit you between the 4th and the 7th. I would also like to invite you and your wife to dinner at night at RIS. I've heard RIS is popular, and I need a reservation at least a week before.

05. Please let me know if you have time to meet me.

06. My email address: ssaito@xxxxx.co.jp

07. I am really looking forward to seeing you for the first time.

08. Sincerely,

09. Shin Saito

✎ 添削

01. ~~Hello~~ Dear Mr. Watson,

02. I'm Shin Saito. I am emailing you because I will be visiting Washington next month to attend the JDEX Expo~~,~~. ~~and~~ I would like to ~~drop~~ come by your company and introduce myself if you are available.

03. I will be in the U.S. from September 2nd to 8th, and ~~I will be free~~ my schedule is quite open ~~after the expo~~ starting on the 4th.

04. If you are available, I would like to visit you at your office sometime between the 4th and the 7th. I would also like to invite you and your wife to dinner ~~at night~~ at RIS. I've heard RIS is popular, and I need a reservation at least a week ~~before~~ in advance.

```
05. Please let me know if you have time to meet me.

06. My email address: ssaito@xxxxx.co.jp

07. I am really looking forward to ~~seeing you for the first time~~ finally meeting you.

08. Sincerely,

09. Shin Saito
```

👉 解説

01 Hello Mr. Watson でも間違いではないのですが、まだ一度も会ったことのない人に宛てたメールであれば、やはり Hello はくだけすぎているかもしれません。Dear が無難です。

02 I am emailing you と目的語を入れることで、単にメールを書いているのではなく、「あなたへメールを差し上げています」という意味になります。

「Expo へ出席すること」と「お会いしたいこと」は分けて書いたほうが、会社への訪問は決してついでなどではなく、とても重要なことであることが伝わります。

drop by 〜 は、「（ランダムな時間に）立ち寄る、顔を出す」という意味なので、フォーマルな訪問であれば、come by（立ち寄る）が適しています。

以下、drop by と come by の用法を、例を挙げて説明します。

［例1］ **I will drop by the office in the afternoon to pick up the document.**

午後に書類を取りにオフィスに立ち寄ります。

Eigobin Pointers　drop by は、おもに「何かを取りに立ち寄るようなちょっとした用事」に言及して使われます。「特に時間を設定しないで、ふらっと立ち寄る」感じです。

［例2］ **I will come by your office around 9 am to see you about the new project.**
新しいプロジェクトについて話したいので、9時ごろにあなたのオフィスに立ち寄ります。

Eigobin Pointers　come by も「立ち寄る」という意味ですが、drop by よりも確実な時間や用件である感じがあります。

03　I will be free（私は暇です）より、my schedule is open（私のスケジュールは空いています）のほうが、フォーマルで、ビジネスメールにふさわしい表現です。

　after the expo であることは前の文から明確なので、それをここでは省略し、代わりに starting on the 4th（4日からはじまり）とします。

04　at your office と追記することで、まずはオフィスへ訪問することが明確になります。

　sometime ～（～のどこかで）を加えることで、「このあいだならどこでもいいですよ」という柔軟性を示すことができます。以下、例文を示します。

［例］ **I'll call you sometime tomorrow night.**
明日の夜（時間はわからないけど）電話します。

　dinner は通常夜なので、at night は不要です。

Eigobin Pointers　ビジネスで初対面の相手への訪問のアポイントメントで、いきなり相手の奥さんを夕食に誘うことは実際にはあまりないと思います。ただし、ビデオカンファレンスなどを通じて事前に、おたがいの家族のことをよく知って

いるというようなことであれば、問題ないと思います。

Eigobin Pointers 講師の書き下ろしバージョンでは、カジュアルに相手の奥さんを夕食に誘うサンプルと、会社への訪問へ焦点を置いたフォーマルなサンプルの両方を用意しました。

ここでは、「事前の予約が必要です」ということが言いたいので、before（〜前に）よりも in advance（前もって）とするべきです。

07 look forward to finally meeting you（ついにお会いできることを楽しみにしております）は、メールや電話でしか面識のない人と対面するときに使われる決まり文句です。

> 添削反映バージョン

Dear Mr. Watson,

I'm Shin Saito. I am emailing you because I will be visiting Washington next month to attend the JDEX Expo. I would like to come by your company and introduce myself if you are available.
I will be in the U.S. from September 2nd to 8th, and my schedule is quite open starting on the 4th.

If you are available, I would like to visit you at your office sometime between the 4th and the 7th. I would also like to invite you and your wife to dinner at RIS. I've heard RIS is popular, and I need a reservation at least a week in advance.

Please let me know if you have time to meet me.

My email address: ssaito@xxxxx.co.jp

I am really looking forward to finally meeting you.

Sincerely,

Shin Saito

同テーマで講師が書き下ろしたバージョン A

※事前にビデオカンファレンスで顔見知りになっていて、相手の奥さん（Debra）も問題なく夕食に誘える間柄である場合のカジュアルなトーンのサンプルです。

Hi Andrew,

Great news!

I will be visiting Washington next month to attend the JDEX Expo so I can finally meet you all in person. The conference is September 2nd to 8th but I can easily make time between the 4th and the 7th. When would be a convenient time for me to come by?

Also, if you can spare an evening, how about I take you and Debra out for dinner at RIS? It would be my great pleasure as a token of appreciation for all of your support over the past two years.

If that's ok with Debra, please let me know your available evenings ASAP and I'll make a reservation.

It will be great to finally see you after all this time.

Regards,

Shin Saito

「同テーマで講師が書き下ろしたバージョンA」語注

□ **in person**「直接に」
　[例]　**I met her a few months ago on the Internet, and next week I'm going to meet her in person for the first time.**
　数ヶ月前にインターネットで彼女に会った。そして初めて直接会う予定になっている。

３人以上で会うときは、all in person「みんなで会う（集まる）」という表現も使えます。

□ **spare**（動詞）「(時間などを)割く」
　[例]　**Can you spare a few minutes?**
　少し時間をとっていただけますか？

□ **as a token of ～**

as a token of appreciation ～ で、「～に対する感謝の印として」という意味になります。
　[例]　**His students gave him a beautiful pen as a token of their appreciation.**

生徒は感謝の印として、彼に美しいペンを贈った。

as a gratitude of 〜 という表現も、「〜に対する感謝の印として」という意味でよく使われます。

> 同テーマで講師が書き下ろしたバージョンＢ

※ビデオカンファレンスのみの知り合いで、あまり親密になっていないため、まずは訪問することを目的としたフォーマルなトーンのサンプルです。

Dear Mr. Watson,

I am very happy to say that I will be in Washington from the 2nd to the 8th of next month for the JDEX Expo.

I would very much like to take the opportunity during this time to come by your office.

My schedule is quite flexible from the 4th through to the 7th so I am happy to work around whatever availability you have.

I am looking forward to finally meeting you in person.

Sincerely,

Shin Saito

「同テーマで講師が書き下ろしたバージョンB」語注

□ **through to** ～「～までずっと」

through to ～ は until ～ と同じ意味ですが、よりフォーマルな文章で、継続性を示すときに使われます。

［例］ **The community center is open through to the end of the year.**
そのコミュニティセンターは年末までずっと開いている。

✉ ビジネスメール ④

お詫び

[メンバー情報]
恵津美様／専門職／34歳

[文の説明]
　台風の影響により印刷工場が浸水し、商品の一部が破損してしまい、納品先の某書店の店長に納期の遅れをお詫びするメールです。

✎ 原文

01. Apology for Delay of Shipment

02. Dear Mr. Taylor,

03. I am a manager of EEE Printing Factory. I apologize for the delay in shipment. After you read this letter, I can understand why you are running out of patience.

04. The big typhoon hit our city yesterday. While we were working, we were urged to evacuate to safer places. After a few hours, our factory was flooded and some merchandise were damaged. The English books which you ordered had already been set, but most of them were gotten soaked.

05. We really understand that that book is so popular and many customers visit your store to get it. Fortunately, since the water was receded early and none of the printers had any problems with operating, we started printing immediately.

We are going to print and send them to you as quickly as possible. We are sure that we should have the books ready to ship within a week.

06. Also, we are going to hold an urgent meeting so soon and discuss how we should protect our merchandise from unforeseen situations, so that the same mistake won't be repeated.

07. Once again, I'm really sorry for the inconvenience.

08. Etsu I

09. EEE Printing Factory Co., Ltd.

✎ 添削

01. Apology for Delay of Shipment

02. Dear Mr. Taylor,

03. I am ~~a~~ the manager of EEE Printing Factory. I apologize for the delay in shipment. ~~After you read this letter, I can understand why you are running out of patience.~~

04. The big typhoon hit our city yesterday. While we were working, we were urged to evacuate to a safer ~~places~~ place.

After a few hours, our factory was flooded and some merchandise ~~were~~ was damaged. The English books which you ordered had already been ~~set~~ packaged and were ready to be sent, but most of them were ~~gotten~~ soaked.

---

05. We really understand that that book is so popular and many customers visit your store to get it. Fortunately, since the water ~~was~~ receded ~~early~~ quickly and none of the printers had any problems ~~with~~ operating, we started printing immediately. We are going to print and send them to you as quickly as possible. We are sure that we ~~should~~ will have the books ready to ship within a week.

---

06. Also, we are going to hold an urgent meeting ~~so soon~~ and discuss how we should protect our merchandise from unforeseen situations, so that the same mistake won't be repeated.

---

07. Once again, I'm really sorry for the inconvenience.

---

08. Etsu I

---

09. EEE Printing Factory Co., Ltd.

☞ 解説

03 今回のようなお詫びのメールは、通常トップ、または責任のある立場の人が送ると思われます。a manager という不定冠詞を使って表記すると、EEE Printing Factory に何人かいるマネージャーのうちの1人を意味する

のに対して、the manager と書くと、EEE Printing Factory のトップマネージャー（または代表する責任者）を指します。ここでは、定冠詞 the を使うか、the general manager のように役職を明確にすることで、読み手の印象がよくなります。

　After you read this letter, I can understand why you are running out of patience. という文は、「この手紙を読んだあと、あなたが立腹される理由が理解できます」という意味で書かれたと思いますが、先方にお詫びを述べるビジネスメールに記されるべき内容ではありません。ここでは省略すべきです。

　04　the typhoon（その台風）は、読み手も周知の大きな台風と思われることから、定冠詞 the を使うことで問題ありませんが、具体的に台風の名前を使うとわかりやすくなります。

　以下、例文を示します。

　　［例1］　**Typhoon Muifa hit our city yesterday.**
　　　　　　台風ムイファーが、私たちの市を直撃しました。

　ここでは、「安全な場所への避難勧告を受けた」という事実を表現しているので、（たとえ複数箇所へ避難していたとしても）safer places ではなく、a safer place（どこかの安全な場所）と不定冠詞を使うほうが自然です。
　また、以下のように簡潔に書くことも可能です。

　　［例2］　**We were urged to evacuate.**
　　　　　　私たちは避難勧告を受けました。

　単語 merchandise は商品・製品を集合として表わしているため、動詞は単数 was を使います。

　単語 set には「準備ができた」という意味がありますが、set はほかにも「固定する、取り付ける、設定する」など広い意味を持つため、あいまいです。

ここでは、packaged and were ready to be sent（梱包され、送るための用意ができていた）と修正することで読み手が理解できるようになります。

Eigobin Pointers 　口語では、I'm all set.（準備できたよ）などと言うことができます。

　were gotten soaked は、英語表現として正しくありません。「水にぬれた」と言う場合は、were soaked、または got soaked のどちらかを使います。

　以下、例文を示します。

［例3］　**The books were soaked.**

［例4］　**The books got soaked.**

05 「水が引いた」は、water receded と能動態で表現できます。受動態にする必要はありません。

　副詞 early は「（定刻より）早く」という意味です。ここでは、「水が素早く引いた」と速度について言及していると思いますので、quickly（速く）を使うべきです。

　単語 problem を用いて「問題がある」と言いたいときは、have problem -ing 〜 または have problem with 〜（物・事柄）のどちらかの表現が使われます。

　「プリンターの稼動について問題はなかった」という表現について、以下両方の例を挙げます。

［例1］　**None of the printers had any problems operating.**

［例2］　**We had no problem with the operation of the printers.**

　ここでは、文を We are sure（私たちは確信しております）という強い表現ではじめ、「1週間以内に準備します」という固い意志をつづける部

分であると思います。ところが、we should ～（私たちは～すべき）と should を使っていることで、後半がまだ検討中であるかのような弱気なトーンになり、全体として不自然な文になっています。should を will ～（～するつもりです）と強いトーンにすることで、統一感のあるはっきりした文になります。

06 an urgent meeting は「緊急のミーティング」という意味で、十分に急いでいることが伝わります。so soon の部分は冗長であり、不要です。

添削反映バージョン

Apology for Delay of Shipment

Dear Mr. Taylor,

I am the manger of EEE Printing Factory. I apologize for the delay in shipment.

The big typhoon hit our city yesterday. While we were working, we were urged to evacuate to a safer place. After a few hours, our factory was flooded and some merchandise was damaged. The English books which you ordered had already been packaged and were ready to be sent, but most of them were soaked.

We really understand that that book is so popular and many customers visit your store to get it. Fortunately, since the water receded quickly and none of the printers had any problems operating, we started printing immediately. We are going to print and send them to you as quickly as possible. We are sure that we will have the books ready to ship within a week.

Also, we are going to hold an urgent meeting and discuss how we should protect our merchandise from unforeseen situations, so that the same mistake won't be repeated.

Once again, I'm really sorry for the inconvenience.

Etsu I
EEE Printing Factory Co., Ltd.

> 同テーマで講師が書き下ろしたバージョン

Apology for Delay of Shipment

Dear Mr. Taylor,

I am the general manager of EEE Printing Factory. I'm afraid we cannot deliver your shipment on time. I truly apologize for this delay.

Typhoon Emily hit our city yesterday. Our factory was flooded and we were forced to evacuate. Some of the copies of the English book which you ordered had already been packaged and were ready to be sent but unfortunately, most of them sustained water damage.

We understand that that book is in high demand and many customers visit your store solely to purchase it. Fortunately, since the water receded quickly and all of the printers were operational, we started reprinting your order immediately. We are going to send them to you as quickly as possible. We are sure that we will have your order ready to ship within a week.

I assure you that we are going to hold an urgent meeting to discuss how we should protect our merchandise from unforeseen situations so that the same situation won't be repeated.

Once again, I'm very sorry for the inconvenience.

Etsu I
EEE Printing Factory Co., Ltd.

「同テーマで講師が書き下ろしたバージョン」語注

☐ **sustain**（動詞）「(損害などを) 受ける、被る」
　[例] **He sustained several injuries from a bicycle accident.**
　　彼は自転車事故で数ヶ所の怪我を負った。

☐ **in high demand**「需要が高い」
　[例] **Since her appearance on television, her CDs have been in high demand.**
　　彼女はテレビに出たおかげで、CDが売れるようになった。

☐ **solely**（副詞）「単に」

[例] **I use a smartphone solely for my business.**
私はスマートフォンを単にビジネス用として使っている。

only, simply, merely も同じ「単に」という意味で使われます。

☐ **unforeseen**（形容詞）「予期しない」

unforeseen circumstances（予期しない事情）/ unforeseen situations（予期しない状況）という組み合わせでよく使われます。

[例] **Barring any unforeseen circumstances, the launch should be July 1st.**
予期しないことが起こらなければ、新製品は7月1日に販売開始の予定です。

ビジネスメール ⑤

注文を出す

[メンバー情報]
K.K. 様／専門職／ 34 歳

[文の説明]
印刷会社への UV 印刷発注のメールです。

✏️ 原文

01. Dear Mr. White,

02. Thank you for sending us a sample of the UV printed smartphone cover.

03. We are thoroughly delighted with the quality of the printing, it recreates the minute color differences of our requested design and the material of the cover that you recommended to be used is also comfortably fitted in hands. We are convinced that this product will meet our discerning customers' taste.

04. We would like to officially place an order as follows.

05. UV printed smartphone cover with design A: 100 unit

06. UV printed smartphone cover with design C: 100 unit

07. Please refer to the attached order sheet in detail.

08. We are now interested in another UV printed items you can offer.

09. Could you send us a list or catalog of the UV printed items that you have made in the past?

10. Yours sincerely,

11. Kanna Komatsu

✍ 添削

01. Dear Mr. White,

02. Thank you for sending us a sample of the UV printed smartphone cover.

03. We are thoroughly delighted with the quality of the printing~~,~~ ~~it~~. It recreates the minute color differences of our requested design and the cover material ~~of the cover~~ that you recommended ~~to be used is also comfortably fitted in hands~~ has a nice feel. We are convinced that this product will meet our discerning customers' ~~taste~~ tastes.

04. We would like to officially place an order ~~as follows~~ for the following.

05. UV printed smartphone cover with design A: 100 ~~unit~~ units

06. UV printed smartphone cover with design C: 100 ~~unit~~ units

07. Please refer to the attached order sheet ~~in detail~~ for details.

08. We are now interested in ~~another~~ other UV printed items you can offer.

09. Could you send us a list or catalog of the UV printed items that you have made in the past?

10. Yours sincerely,

11. Kanna Komatsu

☞ 解説

03　ここでは、「サンプルへの感想」と、「カバーの材質」と話が分かれているので、文を分割します。

　material of the cover は cover material と複合名詞にしたほうが英語らしくなります。

　to be used（使われる）ということは、周知の事実であるため、省略します。「カバーの材質」に対して、comfortably fits in our hands と言うと、「サイズがちょうどいい」という意味になります。「手触りがいい」という表現は、have a nice feel / feel good in our hands / be pleasant to hold といった表現を使います。

　「好み」は人によって異なるので、複数形 tastes を使うのが適切です。

04 「～をオーダーする、～を発注する」は、place an order for ～と for を使います。ここでは as follows を for the following に修正します。

05 **06** カタカナでは「100 ユニット」と表記できますが、複数ある場合は units と複数形を使います。

07 in detail（詳細に）という表現は間違いではないのですが、これは「詳細に見る」という意味にもなります。ここでは「内容の詳細を見るために添付のオーダーシートを確認してください」ということですので、目的の for を使った for details という表現が適しています。

08 another は「もう１つの」という意味で、あとに単数名詞がつづきます。items のように複数名詞がつづく場合は other(その他の)を用います。以下、例を挙げて説明します。

[例1] **I'll buy another computer when this one dies.**
このコンピュータが壊れたら、別のコンピュータを買います。
Eigobin Pointers another を使うことで次のコンピュータは、もう１つの（単数）コンピュータであることがわかります。

[例2] **I've tried other computers, but I don't like any of them.**
他のコンピュータを試してみたけれども、どれもよくなかった。
Eigobin Pointers other computers で、今使っているものとは違う複数のコンピュータであることがわかります。

添削反映バージョン

Dear Mr. White,

Thank you for sending us a sample of the UV printed smartphone cover.

We are thoroughly delighted with the quality of the printing. It recreates the minute color differences of our requested design and the cover material that you recommended has a nice feel. We are convinced that this product will meet our discerning customers' tastes.

We would like to officially place an order for the following.

UV printed smartphone cover with design A: 100 units
UV printed smartphone cover with design C: 100 units

Please refer to the attached order sheet for details.

We are now interested in other UV printed items you can offer. Could you send us a list or catalog of the UV printed items that you have made in the past?

Yours sincerely,

Kanna Komatsu

同テーマで講師が書き下ろしたバージョン

Dear Mr. White,

Thank you for the smartphone cover samples. We were all very impressed with the quality of the printing. We were a little concerned about the color but you got it just right. The material you recommended has a great feel and it seems that it will wear well. We're quite confident that our customers will be very satisfied. Below is our first official order.

UV printed smartphone cover with design A: 100 units
UV printed smartphone cover with design C: 100 units

We are also interested in looking at other UV printed items. Could you send us your most recent catalog along with a price list?

We look forward to doing more business with you in the future.

Sincerely,

Kanna Komatsu

「同テーマで講師が書き下ろしたバージョン」語注

□ **just right**「もってこい、頃合の」
　[例]　**The vegetables were a little overcooked but the steak was just right.**
　野菜は火が通りすぎていたが、ステーキは頃合の焼き具合だった。

□ **wear well**「耐久性がある、長持ちする」
　[例]　**I don't care what brand of shoes you buy as long as they wear well.**
　長持ちするのであれば、どのブランドの靴を買ってもかまわない。

ビジネスメール ⑥

金額を交渉する

[メンバー情報]
英語便 HN：Marie／専門職／39歳

[文の説明]
外国での会議開催にあたり、会場候補のホテルと交渉するメールです。

原文

01. Dear Ms. Baker,

02. Thank you for the quotation for our 'TECH TODAY' conference. I would like to make inquiries about the following items.

03. 1. Transportation
04. Being close to the airport, your hotel is well situated for international meetings. However, it is inconvenient to go to the city center. For the second-day dinner, which is held in the city center, could you please provide free transportation for us, as you usually do for hotel guests?

05. 2. Meeting room
06. The floor plan of the meeting room you chose shows a large empty space at the back of the room. This room seems to be too large for our conference. I would appreciate if you could inform me availability of a smaller room and its renting fee.

07. 3. Room charge
08. As the expense exceeds our budget, could you please consider a discount of 20% because we are booking 150 single rooms for three nights? Also, as another option, we are considering booking 75 twin rooms. would appreciate it if you could also let me know the total room charge of this option.

---

09. I look forward to your reply.

---

10. Sincerely,

---

11. Mari Sato

✍ 添削

01. Dear Ms. Baker,

---

02. Thank you for the quotation for our 'TECH TODAY' conference. I would like to make inquiries about the following ~~items.~~ :

---

03. 1. Transportation
04. Being close to the airport, your hotel is well situated for international meetings. However, it is inconvenient ~~to go to~~ for getting to the city center. ~~For the second day dinner, which is held in the city center~~, We are planning to have dinner in the city center on the second day. Would it be possible for

~~could~~ you ~~please~~ to provide free transportation for us, as you usually do for hotel guests?

---

05. 2. Meeting room
06. The floor plan of the meeting room you chose shows a large empty space at the back of the room. This room seems to be too large for our conference. I would appreciate it if ~~you could inform me availability of~~ we could get a smaller room and also if you could tell me ~~its renting fee~~ how much it will cost to rent.

---

07. 3. Room charge
08. As the expense exceeds our budget, could you please consider a discount of 20% because we are booking 150 single rooms for three nights? Also, as another option, we are considering booking 75 twin rooms. ~~I would appreciate it if you could also~~ Could you let me know the total room charge ~~of~~ for ~~this option~~ both options?

---

09. I look forward to your reply.

---

10. Sincerely,

---

11. Mari Sato

☞ 解説

02 リストを並べて表記するときは、follows や the following のあとに：（コロン）を付けて、項目をつづけます。items は不用です。以下、例を示

します。

[例1] **If your computer freezes, do the following:**
　　　　1. Press Option – Command – Escape to see a list of applications that are running.
　　　　2. Click on whichever application is grayed out.
　　　　3. Click the force quit button.

[例2] **Directions to the party are as follows:**
　　　　1. Catch the #10 bus at the corner of 5th and Main Street.
　　　　2. Get off when the bus turns onto Davis Street. (you'll see a big pink building to your left.)

04　it is inconvenient to go to ～は正しい文ですが、最初の代名詞 it が直前の文のホテルを指しているように思えてしまいます。ホテルに対して動詞の go を使うのは不自然であるため（ホテル自体はどこへも行かないため）、文がわかりにくくなっています。
　ここでは、以下のいずれかの形式に修正する必要があります。

[例1] **However, it is inconvenient to go to the city center from that location/the hotel.**
　　　　しかしながら、そのホテルから都心へ出ることが不便である。

Eigobin Pointers　from that location/the hotel を付け加えて、it が「ホテルから都心まで行くこと」であることを明確にします。

[例2] **However, it is inconvenient to the city center.**
　　　　しかしながら、都心までが、不便である。

Eigobin Pointers　go to を除去して、it がホテルを指していると問題なくわかるようにしています。

[例3] **However, it is inconvenient for getting to the city center.**
　　　　しかしながら、都心へ出るのが不便である。

Eigobin Pointers　for getting to を使うことで、「〜への到達」という意味になります。get to はどうやって到達するかを示す言い方なので、文意に合っています。

　For the second-day dinner ではじまる文は、長すぎて読みにくいので、「夕食をとる予定」と「交通手段について尋ねる」の2つに分割します。
　the second-day dinner は、「2日目の夕食」という日本語をそのまま英語に置き換えただけで、英語として不自然です。これは、dinner on the second day とすべきです。ただし、ここでは、We are planning to have dinner in the city center. と、まず夕食をとることを明確にし、最後に on the second day（2日目に）という情報を付け足します。このほうが自然な文になります。
　Could you please provide free transportation for us?（無料の交通手段をご提供いただけますか？）はていねいで、相手にいい印象を与える文ですが、Would it be possible for you to provide free transportation for us?（無料の交通手段をご提供いただくことは可能でしょうか？）は、さらにていねいな問い合わせの文になります。

06　I would appreciate it if 〜（〜していただければありがたい）ではじまる文は、appreciate（感謝する）が他動詞であるため、目的語の it が必要です。
　「（人に）〜を知らせる」は、inform（人）of [about] 〜 というように、前置詞が必要です。ただし、I would appreciate it if you could inform me of availability of a smaller room.（もう少し小さい部屋の可能性を教えていただければ大変ありがたいです）は、不自然でまわりくどい表現に感じられます。ここでは、はっきり I would appreciate it if we could get a smaller room.（私たちがもう少し小さい部屋が利用できると大変ありがたいです）とすれば、もっとわかりやすくなります。
　renting fee は正しい英語表現ではありません。「借りるのにいくらかかるのか」は、how much it will cost to rent という英語にできます。
　また、前半の inform me の代わりに also if you could tell me を挿入し、〜 also if you could tell me how much it will cost to rent.（また、借り

るのにいくらかかるのか教えていただけますと～）と修正します。

08 「～の料金」は、charge for ～で表現できます。シングルルームとツインルームの両方の場合の料金を知りたいので、both options（両方の選択肢）と修正します。

I would appreciate it if you could also let me know the total room charge for both options. という文は英語としては完璧ですが、ここでは相手に何かの手配をお願いしているのではなく、単に値段を尋ねているだけなので、もっとはっきりした言い方にできます。以下、例を示します。

[例] **Could you let me know** the total room **charge for both options**?
両方のオプションの部屋代を教えていただけますか？

添削反映バージョン

Dear Ms. Baker,

Thank you for the quotation for our 'TECH TODAY' conference. I would like to make inquiries about the following:

1. Transportation
Being close to the airport, your hotel is well situated for international meetings. However, it is inconvenient for getting to the city center. We are planning to have dinner in the city center on the second day. Would it be possible for you to provide free transportation for us, as you usually do for hotel guests?

2. Meeting room
The floor plan of the meeting room you chose shows a large empty space at the back of the room. This room seems to be too large for our conference. I would appreciate it if we could get a smaller room and also if you could tell me how much it will cost to rent.

3. Room charge
As the expense exceeds our budget, could you please consider a discount of 20% because we are booking 150 single rooms for three nights? Also, as another option, we are considering booking 75 twin rooms. Could you let me know the total room charge for both options?

I look forward to your reply.

Sincerely,

Mari Sato

同テーマで講師が書き下ろしたバージョン

Dear Ms. Baker,

Thank you so much for the quotation for our 'TECH TODAY' conference. There are a few things I would like to ask you about:

1. Transportation to downtown
Although it's nice that your hotel is located near the airport, it's rather inconvenient if you want to go downtown. We are planning on having dinner downtown on our second day and I'm wondering how we can get everyone there. Is the free shuttle bus to downtown service available for large groups?

2. Meeting room size
I'm afraid the conference room you recommended for us is far too big for our needs. We're looking for something smaller so we don't have to mess with a PA system. In your brochure, there is a picture of a room that looks about half the size. Is it available? How much would it cost?

3. Room charge
Your quotation is somewhat higher than our budget allows. Would it be possible to get a 20% discount because we are also booking 150 single rooms? I'm also wondering if it might be cheaper to book 75 twin rooms instead. Could you tell me your best rate for both options?

I hope to hear from you soon.

Sincerely,

Mari Sato

「同テーマで講師が書き下ろしたバージョン」語注

□ **need**（名詞）「ニーズ、必要性」

通常 needs と複数形で使われます。too ～ for one's needs で、「必要性に対して～すぎる」という意味になります。

[例] **This camera is too complicated for my needs.**
　　　このカメラは私の必要性に対して複雑すぎる。

□ **PA system**（public-address system）（名詞）「拡声装置」

PA だけでもよく使われます。

[例] **Who is setting up the PA?**
　　　誰が拡声装置をセッティングするのですか？

✉ ビジネスメール ⑦

招待する

[メンバー情報]
和田　憲和様／翻訳家／28歳

[文の説明]
社外コンサルタントを年末パーティに招待するメールです。

✎ 原文

01. Dear Michael Methe,

02. Thank you for your insightful consultation to our corporation as usual.

03. This time we are truly honored to invite you to the year-end party for our business partners.

04. The details are as follows:
05. Date: December 19, 2011
06. Time: 19:00- 21:00
07. Location: Umeda Park Building 8F in Osaka (the map is attached in this e-mail)
08. Fee: Free

09. If it's convenient for you, Minako Nakano and I would like to invite you the second bar.

10. If you have any suggestions about where to go, please feel

free to let us know.

11. We are really looking forward to meeting with you.

12. Warm regards,

13. Norikazu Wada

✍️ 添削

01. Dear Michael Methe,

02. Thank you for your continued insightful consultation ~~to our corporation as usual~~.

03. ~~This time~~ At this time we are truly honored to invite you to the year-end party for our business partners.

04. The details are as follows:
05. Date: December 19, 2011
06. Time: 19:00- 21:00
07. Location: Umeda Park Building 8F in Osaka (the map is attached in this e-mail)
08. Fee: Free

09. If it's convenient for you, Minako Nakano and I would like to invite you ~~the second bar~~ out for a drink after the party.

10. If you have any suggestions about where to go, please ~~feel free to~~ let us know.

11. We are really looking forward to ~~meeting with~~ seeing you.

12. Warm regards,

13. Norikazu Wada

👉 解説

02 as usual（いつものように）は、ビジネスのお礼として使うには、くだけすぎた表現です。ここでは「継続した」という意味の continued を使ったほうがいいし、そのほうがていねいに聞こえます。

　to our corporation（我が社にとって）の部分は文脈から明らかなため、省略することができます。

03 this time という表現は、「今回は」または「今度こそは」という意味になり、今回が何か特別なパーティ（はじめてのパーティ、いままでとは違う趣旨のパーティなど）であるかのように聞こえてしまいます。this time の用法について例を挙げて説明します。

[例1] **I am going to Hokkaido again, and this time I am going to Muroran.**

　　　北海道へまた行くつもりです。そして、今回は（今度こそは）室蘭に行く予定です。

Eigobin Pointers　北海道へは過去に行ったことがあるが、室蘭へ行くのははじめて、または何かの理由で長いあいだ室蘭へ行くことができなかったような印象を

与えます。

　招待のメールでは、this time ではなく、at this time と前置詞 at を加えることで、「この時期に」という意味になり、忘年会の話に自然につながるようになります。

Eigobin Pointers　また、もっと具体的に、this December（この12月）, this winter（この冬）というような表現を使うこともできます。

　At this time we are truly honored to invite you to the year-end party for our business partners. という説明だけでは、やや情報が不十分に聞こえます。

　year-end party に関する具体的情報を補足することで、招待を受け取った相手がパーティをイメージしやすくなります。以下、例文を示します。

[例2]　**the year-end party that our management is hosting for our business partners**

　　　私たちの経営者がビジネスパートナー様のために主催する忘年会

Eigobin Pointers　読み手が、会社の忘年会とは違う、特別に企画されたパーティに招待されていることがわかります。

[例3]　**year-end party for our staff and business partners**

　　　私たちのスタッフとビジネスパートナー様のための忘年会

Eigobin Pointers　読み手が、会社のスタッフの忘年会に招待されていることが理解できます。

09　the second bar は「2次会」という意味合いで書かれていると思います。 文法的には問題ないのですが、2次会は日本の風習であり、海外の人には意味が通じない可能性もあります。なので、out for a drink after the party という言い方が適しています。

Eigobin Pointers　out for a drink afterwards「あとで飲みに行く」という言い方もよく使われます。out for a drink after the party よりややくだけた表現になります。

10　If you have any suggestions, please feel free to let us know. は、

「何かご提案があれば何なりとお知らせください」というつもりで書かれていると思われますが、feel free to 〜（自由に〜する）という表現は、どちらかというと「相手に〜してもらいたい」というニュアンスを含んでしまうため、読み手は「２次会の場所に関して、何か提案しなくちゃいけない？」とある種のプレッシャーを感じてしまうかもしれません。

ここでは、feel free to を外して、If you have any suggestions, let us know. とするのがいいと思います。

反対に、「相手に〜してもらいたい」という場面では、feel free to 〜, don't hesitate to 〜といった表現が適しています。以下、例を挙げて説明します。

[例1]　**If you have any questions, please feel free to contact me.**
何かご質問がございましたら、自由に私へご連絡ください。

[例2]　**If you are interested in our products, please don't hesitate to contact me.**
私たちの製品にご興味がありましたら、遠慮なく私へご連絡ください。

11　動詞 meet には、「紹介される（はじめて会う）」という意味合いがあるため、I'm looking forward to meeting you. は、「（はじめて）お会いできることを楽しみにしています」というニュアンスになってしまいます。

ここでは、see を使って、I'm looking forward to seeing you. とするのが適当です。

Eigobin Pointers　I'm looking forward to seeing you. を、はじめて会う人に対して使うことは問題ありません。

添削反映バージョン

Dear Michael Methe,

Thank you for your continued insightful consultation.
At this time we are truly honored to invite you to the year-end party for our business partners.

The details are as follows:
Date: December 19, 2011
Time: 19:00- 21:00
Location: Umeda Park Building 8F in Osaka (the map is attached in this e-mail)
Fee: Free

If it's convenient for you, Minako Nakano and I would like to invite you out for a drink after the party.
If you have any suggestions about where to go, please let us know.

We are really looking forward to seeing you.

Warm regards,

Norikazu Wada

同テーマで講師が書き下ろしたバージョン

Dear Michael Methe,

Thank you for your continued contributions towards our corporation's success.

This December, management is hosting an end-of-year party for our valued business partners. We would be truly honored if you could join us at that time.

The details are as follows:
* Date: December 19, 2011
* Time: 19:00- 21:00
* Location: Umeda Park Building 8F in Osaka (the map is in the attachment)

If convenient, Minako Nakano and I would like to take you out for a drink after the party concludes.
Please let us know if you have any requests regarding a bar. Otherwise, we will take you to one of our favorites.
We are really looking forward to seeing you.

Warm regards,

Norikazu Wada

「同テーマで講師が書き下ろしたバージョン」語注

□ **management**（名詞）「経営者（側）」

集団としての経営者 management に対しては、staff（社員、スタッフ［側］）が使われます。

［例］　**Management has changed the policy for paid vacations.**
　　　経営サイドは有給休暇に関する方針を変更した。

□ **truly honored**「大変光栄に思っている」

［例］　**Nancy said she was truly honored to be named the employee of the month.**
　　　ナンシーは、今月の社員に選ばれたことを大変光栄に思っていると言った。

何かを受賞したときのスピーチでは、I am truly honored.（大変光栄に思っております）というセリフがよく使われます。

□ **conclude**（動詞）「終わる」

会議やセミナーなど、公式な場が終わるときにおもに使われます。

［例］　**When the Q&A session concludes, there will be refreshments in a lobby.**
　　　Q&Aセッション終了後には、ロビーに軽食を用意してあります。

✉ ビジネスメール ⑧

クレーム

[メンバー情報]
A.C. 様／その他／35 歳

[文の説明]
品物（段ボール箱）の納品が非常に遅れたうえに、サイズと数が違って納品されていた、しかも前回にも同じようなミスがあったことに苦情を述べるメールです。

✏ 原文

---

01. Dear Richard Blaine, Head of Marketing

---

02. This is Akiko Chiba, Sales Manager of Star Airlines. I'm writing to you to express our complaint against your dishonest business.

---

03. We ordered 1,000 cardboard boxes (Large size 200, Medium one 500 and Small one 300) on 12th July. We finally received them yesterday; we had to wait more than two weeks for them! What matters worse is there were mistakes about the number of each size; you sent us: Large 100, Medium 600 and Small 300.

---

04. We are in trouble so much. The lack of cardboard boxes has already brought our business some serious obstacles.

---

05. In addition to that, in the previous order, there was the same

mistake. We informed the chief of the department about that by e-mail, but we couldn't even receive a reply.

06. Your attitude lacks honesty so much and damages our relationship based on confidence. We have been thinking about stopping dealing with your office.

07. Anyway, could you check our last order and send the boxes again as soon as possible? I expect you to cope with your mistake faithfully.

08. Best regards,

09. Akiko Chiba

添削

01. Dear Richard Blaine, ~~Head of Marketing~~

02. This is Akiko Chiba, Sales Manager of Star Airlines. I'm writing to you ~~to express our complaint against your dishonest business~~ to complain about the poor service we have experienced.

03. We ordered 1,000 cardboard boxes (Large size 200, Medium ~~one~~ ones 500 and Small ~~one~~ ones 300) on the 12th of July. We finally received them yesterday; we had to wait more than two weeks for them! What matters worse is the number

was wrong. ~~there~~ There were mistakes ~~about the number of each size~~ regarding size; you sent us: Large 100, Medium 600 and Small 300.

04. We are in ~~trouble~~ so much trouble. The lack of cardboard boxes has already brought our business some serious obstacles.

05. In addition to that, in the previous order, there was the same mistake. We informed the chief of the department about that by e-mail, but we couldn't even receive a reply.

06. ~~Your attitude lacks honesty so much~~ This is unacceptable and damages our relationship which is based on confidence. We have been thinking about stopping dealing with your office.

07. Anyway, could you check our last order and send the boxes again as soon as possible? I expect you to cope with your mistake faithfully.

08. ~~Best regards,~~ Yours sincerely,

09. Akiko Chiba

👉 解説

01 Dear ではじまるあて先の名前のあとに、役職を入れるのはあまり一般的な書き方ではありません。ここでは削除したほうがいいでしょう。

Eigobin Pointers　相手の担当者の名前がわからないようなときは、送付する封筒のあて先や、レターのヘッダーに Attention: (省略形 Attn: / ATTN:) を使って役職を記述することができます。

［例］　**Attn: Head of Marketing**
　　　　KKK Co. Ltd.

02　express our complaint という言い方は不自然な英語表現です。苦情を述べる場合には、普通、以下のような言い方をします。

［例1］　**We have a complaint with ～**
　　　　〜に関して苦情があります

［例2］　**I'm writing to you to complain about ～**
　　　　〜に対して苦情を言うために書いています

また、相手方の行為に対して不快感を示すときは、以下のような表現も可能です。

［例3］　**We are displeased with the actions of ～**
　　　　〜に対して、気分を害しております

dishonest business（いいかげんなビジネス）という表現は、通常あまり使われません。大変強いトーンで、読み手には中傷ととられる可能性もあります。ここでは、**to complain about the poor service we have experienced**（私たちが経験した不十分なサービスに苦情を言うために）といった表現が適切です。

03　cardboard boxes は複数あるため、ones と複数形を使います。
　July 12th、または、July 12 といった表記は、略式として実際に使われていますが、正式な表記は、the 12th of July という形になります。会社

間のフォーマル文では、正式な表記を使うのが無難です。

What matters worse ～（さらに悪いことに）ではじまる文は、長すぎて、意味がわかりにくくなっています。What matters worse is the number was wrong.（さらに悪いことに数を間違えています）と、まず結論を述べてから、詳細説明に入ると、わかりやすくなります。

mistakes about the number of each size は英語として正しい表現ですが、今回は3サイズのうち、2つのサイズの個数が誤っていたということなので、each size（それぞれのサイズ）という表現は厳密に正しくなくなります。なので、ここでは mistakes regarding size（サイズに関しての誤り）として、もう少し広い意味で表現するのがいいでしょう。

04　「多くのトラブル」と言う場合、通常 so much trouble という表現を使います。以下、例文を示します。

　［例］　**I will be in so much trouble if I don't get this done today.**
　　　　もし今日やらなかったら大変なことになる。

06　Your attitude lacks honesty（あなたの態度は誠実さに欠けています）という表現も、相手に「中傷」ととられてしまう危険性があります。This is unacceptable（これは容認できません）とすることで、相手への中傷ではなく、自分の許しがたい気持ちを表現することができます。

関係代名詞が目的格のときは省略できますが、主格の場合は省略できません。ここでは、relationship が主格であるため、関係代名詞 which が必要です。以下、例を挙げて説明します。

　［例1］　関係代名詞が主格の場合
　　　　　The woman who lives next door, was on holiday.
　Eigobin Pointers　関係代名詞 who が必要です。

　［例2］　関係代名詞が目的格の場合
　　　　　The woman（who/that）I wanted to see was on holiday.

> **Eigobin Pointers** 関係代名詞 (who/that) は省略できます。

08 Best regards は「よろしく」という感じのカジュアルな挨拶ですので、今回のような苦情のメールのトーンに合いません。ビジネスレターの固い結びには、Yours sincerely（敬具）が適しています。

添削反映バージョン

Dear Richard Blaine,

This is Akiko Chiba, Sales Manager of Star Airlines. I'm writing to you to complain about the poor service we have experienced.

We ordered 1,000 cardboard boxes (Large size 200, Medium ones 500 and Small ones 300) on the 12th of July. We finally received them yesterday; we had to wait more than two weeks for them! What matters worse is the order was wrong. There were mistakes regarding size; you sent us: Large 100, Medium 600 and Small 300.

We are in so much trouble. The lack of cardboard boxes has already brought our business some serious obstacles.

In addition to that, in the previous order, there was the same mistake. We informed the chief of the department about that by e-mail, but we couldn't even receive a reply.

This is unacceptable and damages our relationship which is based on confidence. We have been thinking about stopping dealing with your office.

Anyway, could you check our last order and send the boxes again as soon as possible? I expect you to cope with your mistake faithfully.

Yours sincerely,

Akiko Chiba

同テーマで講師が書き下ろしたバージョン

Dear Mr Blaine,

This is Akiko Chiba, Sales Manager of Star Airlines. I'm writing to formally complain about your company's recent performance.

We recently ordered 1,000 cardboard boxes (large 200; medium 500; small 300) on the 12th of July. We received them yesterday, after a delay of over two weeks. To make matters worse, there were mistakes regarding size. We received, large 100; medium 600; small 300.

The delay in this shipment has caused Star Airlines a great many problems. Moreover, this is not an isolated case. In the previous order there were also errors concerning quantity. On that occasion we informed the chief of the department by email but did not even receive the courtesy of a reply.

Mr Blaine, if we are to continue to do business with your company we need you to ensure that these kinds of situations never occur again.

Could you check our last order and forward the unsent boxes as soon as possible?

I look forward to your prompt reply.

Yours sincerely,

Akiko Chiba

「同テーマで講師が書き下ろしたバージョン」語注

☐ **isolate**（動詞）「分離する」

isolated 〜 で「（本題から離れた）別の〜」という意味の形容詞になります。

［例］ **Although the war is over, there have been isolated incidents of fighting in some areas.**

戦争が終了したにもかかわらず、ある地域では別の戦闘が起きている。

☐ **courtesy**（名詞）「礼儀、親切」

［例］ **Do you think that the younger generation lacks common courtesy?**

若い世代は一般的な礼儀を欠いていると思いますか？

☐ **prompt**（形容詞）「迅速な」

a prompt reply で「即答」という意味になります。

[例] **A prompt reply to an email leaves a really good impression.**
Eメールの迅速な返信は、相手にいい印象を与える。

ビジネス文書 ①

年頭の挨拶と商品について

[メンバー情報]
K.M. 様／その他／38 歳

[文の説明]
　弊社（ジュエリー販売会社）から顧客企業への新年の挨拶と、ある商品に関する重要な情報を知らせるビジネス文書です。

✏️ 原文

01. A Happy New Year.

02. We appreciate your continued business last year.

03. At the beginning of a new year, we are delighted to announce that we will introduce some new cuts and new colors of our stones in October.

04. Our development team in Switzerland has long been struggled for innovation for these three years and their effort finally get done as things.

05. Moreover, as an answer to customer's requests, we decided to launch new colors for the first time in decades. Lastly, we have added a polishing process one more stage so that it makes a stone more shine. We strongly believe that people those see our stones will believe they are real and will be surprised that they are synthetic.

06. Regrettably, we also have to announce this news. We have kept stone price for these three years due to our restructuring and automation. But, we can not afford the increasing costs of labor, shipping and materials anymore. Especially, unique colored stone is few and therefore it becomes higher. All things considered, we will change our price in April. Please understand this situation and we appreciate your patience.

---

07. We hope that we can keep our good relationship as same as before.

✍️ 添削

01. ~~A~~ Happy New Year.

---

02. We appreciate your continued business last year.

---

03. At the beginning of a new year, we are delighted to announce that we will introduce some new cuts and ~~new~~ colors of our stones in October.

---

04. Our development team in Switzerland has long been ~~struggled for innovation for these three years and their effort finally get done as things~~ intensively researching new products for the past three years, resulting in these new products and their efforts have recently been rewarded.

---

05. Moreover, as an answer to ~~customer's~~ customer requests, we decided to launch new colors for the first time in decades. Lastly, we have added ~~a~~ another polishing process ~~one more stage~~ so that it makes a stone ~~more shine~~ shine more. We strongly believe that ~~people~~ those who see our stones will believe they are real and will be surprised that they are synthetic.

06. Regretfully, we also have to announce this news. We ~~have kept stone price for these three years~~ have been able to keep our stone prices low for the past three years due to our restructuring and automation. But, we ~~can not~~ cannot afford the increasing costs of labor, shipping and materials anymore. ~~Especially, unique~~ Unique colored ~~stone is~~ stones are especially ~~few~~ rare and therefore ~~it becomes higher~~ more expensive. All things considered, we will change our price in April. Please understand this situation and we appreciate your patience.

07. We hope that we can keep our good relationship ~~as~~ the same as before.

👉 解説

01 日本語では、「謹賀新年」など名詞で新年の挨拶を書くことがありますが、英語では通常 A Happy New Year という名詞形ではなく、冠詞を外して、Happy New Year、または Wishing you a Happy New Year と挨拶として書くのが一般的です。

03　new cuts and new colors と同じ形容詞を使っているときは、new cuts and colors と2番目の形容詞を省略できます。

04　「奮闘しています」という意味では、been struggled という受動態ではなく、been struggling と進行形を使います。ただし、the team has long been struggling という表現は、社員が大変な苦労をしているという少々ネガティブな表現になります。「懸命に頑張っていた結果、苦労が報われた」というポジティブなイメージを出すのであれば、以下のような表現が適しています。

[例]　**Our development team in Switzerland has long been intensively researching new products for the past three years, resulting in these new products and their efforts have recently been rewarded.**
　　われわれのスイスの開発チームは、過去3年間、新製品の研究に注力してまいりました。その結果、こうした新製品が生まれ、開発チームの努力が最近になってようやく報われました。

05　顧客の要求は customer requests と複合名詞で表現することができます。
　we have added a polishing process one more stage という表現は、a polishing stage（つや出しの段階）と、one more stage（そのほかにもう1つの段階）の両方を追加したように聞こえる可能性があります。「別のつや出しの工程を追加した」という意味であれば、we have added another polishing process とすれば、読み手にすんなり理解してもらえます。
　ここでは shine（輝く）は動詞なので、more shine とすると誤りです。副詞の more を動詞のうしろに付けて、shine more（もっと輝く）としましょう。
　people と those はここでは、両方とも「人びと」を指すため、両方は必要ありません。以下のどちらかに修正します。

[例1]　〜 **people who take a glance** 〜
[例2]　〜 **those who take a glance** 〜

06　We have kept stone price（石の価格を保ってきた）につづけて、at 〜（いくらで）という情報が必要となります。「リストラとオートメーションにより、石の価格を低価格に保つことができている」と言う場合は、low（[価格が] 低い）と be able to（〜できている）を加え、We have been able to keep our stone prices low 〜 とすれば、意味が通じます。

　can not は通常、cannot と 1 語で書くか、または can't と短縮形にするのが一般的です。

Eigobin Pointers　ただし、以下のように not が他のフレーズに含まれている場合には、can not と 2 語で記述します。

[例1]　**He can not only sing but dance.**
　　　　彼は歌えるだけでなくダンスもできる。

Eigobin Pointers　not が、not only 〜 but 〜のフレーズの一部になっています。

　日本語で「特に〜」で文がはじまる場合、どうしても especially を頭に持っていってしまいますが、英語では especially が文頭で使われることはないので、注意しましょう。especially は、普通は動詞の前で使われます。be 動詞の場合は、動詞のあとで使われます。

　以下、especially を使った例文を示します。

[例2]　**I especially love chocolate.**
　　　　特にチョコレートが大好きです。

　形容詞 many, few は、限定用法（few people のような形容詞＋名詞の用法）では使えますが、叙述用法（〜 is few のように、補語に単独で使われる用法）では使えません。ここでは、few の代わりに、rare（数少ない、まれな）を使うことができます。

　The price is high.（価格が高い）のように、high は price などの補語と

して「(価格が)高い」という意味で用いますが、high だけでは「価格が高い」という意味になりません。ここでは、expensive(高価な)を使います。

07 same は一般的に the を付けて使用し、as same as ではなく、the same as とします。以下、例文を示します。

[例]　**Your new phone looks the same as your old one.**
　　　あなたの新しい電話は、古いものと同じように見える。

添削反映バージョン

Happy New Year.

We appreciate your continued business last year.

At the beginning of a new year, we are delighted to announce that we will introduce some new cuts and colors of our stones in October. Our development team in Switzerland has long been intensively researching new products for the past three years, resulting in these new products and their efforts have recently been rewarded.

Moreover, as an answer to customer requests, we decided to launch new colors for the first time in decades. Lastly, we have added another polishing process so that it makes a stone shine more. We strongly believe that those who see our stones will believe they are real and will be surprised that they are synthetic.

Regrettably, we also have to announce this news. We have been able to keep our stone prices low for the past three years due to our restructuring and automation. But, we cannot afford the increasing costs of labor, shipping and materials anymore. Unique colored stones are especially rare and therefore more expensive. All things considered, we will change our price in April. Please understand this situation and we appreciate your patience.

We hope that we can keep our good relationship the same as before.

同テーマで講師が書き下ろしたバージョン

Happy New Year.

Thank you for your continued support during the past year.

At the beginning of a new year, we are delighted to announce that we will introduce a new range of synthetic diamonds from October. Our development team in Switzerland has succeeded in creating some new cutting and polishing technology. In addition, in response to customer requests, we have decided to launch a new range of colors. We strongly believe that our coming range of stones will be indistinguishable from the genuine article to the naked eye.

Regrettably, however, we must also give notice of a slight increase in price. We have been able to keep our stone prices low for the past three years due to restructuring and automation, but we cannot continue to absorb the increasing costs of labor, shipping and materials from our Asian production facilities. We will be announcing our new price list in April. We hope you can appreciate the necessity for the price rise which we will endeavor to keep as minimal as possible.

We look forward to serving you again during the coming twelve months.

「同テーマで講師が書き下ろしたバージョン」語注

- **indistinguishable**（形容詞）「区別がつかない、見分けがつかない」
  - [例] These days one computer is indistinguishable from another.
    近頃は、どのコンピュータも見分けがつかない。

- **absorb**（動詞）「吸収する、負担する」
  - [例] We have to absorb the price increase of the material.
    われわれは、原材料の値上げを吸収しなければならない。

ビジネス文書 ②

新製品の発表

[メンバー情報]
室園　靖様／技術職／33歳

[文の説明]
工場で使う新製品ロボットのアナウンスです。

原文

01. Announcement of new product : EB-V01

02. ABC Electronics Inc. today announced the EB-V01 system, a full-function verbal interpreter for ABC's 32-bit manufacturing robots. Priced at $1,500, the EB-V01 supports the company's popular V10 family with speeds up to double. The system enables system designers to give complex input for manufacturing robots by directly speaking instead of time-consuming programming, at a significantly reduced cost.

03. With the EB-V01 system, we are delivering a very efficient microphone at cheap cost for a wide range of customers. Customers can reduce overall development costs and time to market for their products. Additionally, from small to mid-size companies can afford to buy our system compared to alternative manufacturing robot that often is more expensive and less efficient.

✍ 添削

01. New Product Announcement ~~of new product~~ : EB-V01

---

02. ABC Electronics Inc. today officially announced the EB-V01 system, a full-function verbal interpreter for ABC's 32-bit manufacturing robots. Priced at $1,500, the EB-V01 supports the company's popular V10 family with speeds up to ~~double~~ twice as fast. The system enables system designers to give complex ~~input~~ commands ~~for~~ to manufacturing robots by directly speaking instead of time-consuming programming, at a significantly reduced cost.

---

03. With the EB-V01 system, we are delivering a ~~very~~ more efficient microphone at ~~cheap~~ a lower cost for a wide range of customers. Customers can substantially reduce overall development costs and time to market ~~for their products~~. Additionally, ~~from small to mid-size companies can afford to buy our system~~ the EB-V01 system is more affordable for smaller companies, especially compared to alternative manufacturing ~~robot~~ robots that are often ~~is~~ more expensive and less efficient.

☞ 解説

01 Announcement of new product は「新製品の発表」を英訳したものと思いますが、of を除いて、New product announcement と短くすることができます。また、目立つように New Product Announcement とタイトルの語頭を大文字にしてもいいでしょう。

また、タイトルは以下のように直接的に書くこともできます。

[例]　**Introducing the EB-V01**
　　　EB-V01 のご紹介

02　officially を加えることで、正式な発表を意味します。
　speed up to double は正しい英語表現ではありません。「２倍速までの速さ」は up to twice as fast とします。
　input（入力）という表現は、（どんな情報にも当てはまってしまうため）あいまいです。ロボットに与える命令であれば、command（命令、指示）が適しています。

Eigobin Pointers　「インプット / アウトプット」はカタカナでもよく使われるものですが、海外では日本ほど頻繁に使われていません。ビジネス文書では、誤解を避けるために、できるだけ具体的な表現を使いましょう。

　「〜に command を送る」は、give command to 〜 とします。

03　very efficient では、具体的にどのような変化があるのかわかりにくいので、以下どちらかのようにする必要があります。

[例1]　**We are delivering a more efficient microphone.**
　　　さらに効率のいいマイクを供給しています。
Eigobin Pointers　前バージョンと比べてマイクの効率が上がっていることを説明しています。

[例2]　**We are delivering very sensitive microphone.**
　　　ものすごく感度のいいマイクを供給しています。
Eigobin Pointers　マイクの効率について具体的に言及しています。

Eigobin Pointers　we are delivering（供給しています）と言うと、マイクは製品に同梱されていることになります。マイクが別売りである場合は、we are offering（提供しています）とすべきです。

単語 cheap はビジネス文書で使うにはややくだけすぎていて、不適切です。

　ここでは low を使い、さらに lower と比較級を使うことで、「（以前より）コストが下がった」という点を強調することができます。

　単に、reduce overall development costs（全体的な開発コストを削減する）とするよりも、substantially（大幅に）を加えることで、substantially reduce overall development costs（全体的な開発コストを大幅に削減する）と効果を強調することができます。

　for their products は、文脈から判断できるので、ここでは必要ありません。

　from small to mid-size companies can afford to buy our system（中小企業が私たちのシステムを購入することができる）とするよりも、製品名を主語にして、the EB-V01 system is more affordable for smaller companies（EB-V01 システムは小さい企業に対しても、さらにお手頃になっている）とすることで、そのよい点について言及していることが明確になります。

　ここではロボット全般を指しているので、複数形の robots を使います。

添削反映バージョン

New Product Announcement : EB-V01

ABC Electronics Inc. today officially announced the EB-V01 system, a full-function verbal interpreter for ABC's 32-bit manufacturing robots. Priced at $1,500, the EB-V01 supports the company's popular V10 family with speeds up to twice as fast. The system enables system designers to give complex commands to manufacturing robots by directly speaking instead of time-consuming programming, at a significantly reduced cost.

With the EB-V01 system, we are delivering a more efficient microphone, at a lower cost for a wide range of customers. Customers can substantially reduce overall development costs and time to market. Additionally, the EB-V01 system is more affordable for smaller companies, especially compared to alternative manufacturing robots that are often more expensive and less efficient.

> 同テーマで講師が書き下ろしたバージョン

New Product Announcement: EB-V01

ABC Electronics Inc. announces the release of the EB-V01 system, a full-function verbal interpreter for ABC's 32-bit manufacturing robots. The EB-V01 is the latest in our series of interpreters that enable system designers to give complex commands to manufacturing robots through voice commands instead of time-consuming programming. Priced at $1,500, the EB-V01 supports the company's popular V10 family of manufacturing robots, with speeds up to twice as fast as existing models.

With the EB-V01, we are delivering a more efficient microphone along with a cost effective interpreting system that will help companies substantially reduce overall development costs and time to market.

> It will enable a greater range of companies to take advantage of voice command robot technology.

「同テーマで講師が書き下ろしたバージョン」語注

☐ **existing**（形容詞）「現在の、現行の」

[例] **In most countries, the existing laws for Internet privacy are insufficient.**

ほとんどの国で、現行のインターネットプライバシーに関する法律は不十分である。

「現在の、現行の」という意味では、他に present, current も同様に使えます。

☐ **time to** ～「～するまでの時間」

time to market で「製品化（商品化）までの時間」という意味になります。time to launch（新製品を売り出すまでの時間）, time to delivery（納期）などもビジネスでよく使われる表現です。

[例] **In the tech industry, time to market is getting shorter and shorter.**

技術産業では、製品化までの時間はどんどん短くなっている。

ビジネス文書 ③

開催延期のお知らせ

[メンバー情報]
M.M様／会社員／42歳

[文の説明]
参加者不足で、Eメール管理のセミナーが延期になったという通知です。

原文

01. Information about working seminar in April

02. The next working seminar in April will be postponed because we couldn't receive enough applicants for the seminar.

03. I am sorry for the inconvenience.

04. We will promptly refund for all applicants who already paid for the seminar. The next seminar will be held in June. We will inform you the date and details as soon as a decision is made.

05. Please contact us if you have any questions.

06. Thank you for the cooperation and understanding.

07. Miki Morita

✍ 添削

01. Information ~~about~~ regarding ~~working~~ email management seminar in April

---

02. The next ~~working~~ email management seminar in April ~~will be~~ has been postponed because ~~we couldn't receive~~ there weren't enough applicants ~~for the seminar~~.

---

03. ~~I am~~ We are sorry for the inconvenience.

---

04. ~~We~~ Applicants who have already paid for the seminar will ~~promptly~~ receive a refund ~~for all applicants who already paid for the seminar.~~ The next seminar will be ~~held~~ scheduled in June. ~~We will inform you the~~ The date and details will be posted as soon as a decision is made.

---

05. Please contact ~~us~~ Human Resources if you have any questions.

---

06. Thank you for ~~the~~ your cooperation and understanding.

---

07. Miki Morita

☞ 解説

01 about でも間違いではありませんが、regarding を使うことで、ビジネス文書に適したトーンになります。

　working seminar という表記は、読み手には通じているのかもしれませ

んが、具体的に何のセミナーであるのかイメージできません。たとえば、email management seminar（Eメール管理セミナー）などと内容に関する情報を付加することで、より明確になります。

　セミナーの日程は「未来」に予定されているものですが、「延期されること」はすでに決定しています。ここでは現在完了形を使って、has been postponed（延期されました）とすべきです。

　we couldn't receive enough applicants（十分な数の応募者を集めることができなかった）とすると、「（たとえ事実であっても）自分たちの能力・努力不足でできなかった」という意味になってしまいます。単に、「参加者が十分ではなかった」という事実を伝えるのであれば、there weren't enough applicants（十分な数の参加者がいなかった）とすれば十分です。

　for the seminar（セミナーへの）は文脈から明らかなので、不要です。

03　I am sorry ～としてしまうと、個人的にお詫びしているようなトーンになります。会社としてのお詫びであれば、We are sorry ～が適当です。

04　We will promptly refund ...（われわれは直ちにご返金いたします）と、自分たちを主語にするのではなく、読み手を主語にし、Applicants who have already paid for the seminar will receive a refund.（セミナーの代金をすでにお支払いされた応募者は、払い戻しを受けます）とすることで、読み手は返金を受けられることが明確になります。

　以下のような文も、読み手（顧客）を主語にすることで、読み手がどんな利益が受けられるか、明確に伝わります。

　　［例1］　**Customers who** hold a point card will receive a 5% discount on the first day of every month.
　　　　　ポイントカード持参のお客様は、毎月1日に5％の割引になります。

　　［例2］　**Passengers who** are willing to take the later flight will receive an upgrade to business class.

後続のフライトをご利用希望のお客様は、ビジネスクラスへの変更が可能です。

will be held（開催される）はまったく問題ないのですが、まだ具体的な日付や詳細が決定されていない場合は、will be scheduled（予定されています）としたほうがいいでしょう。

　ここでも、自分たちを主語にするのではなく、重要な情報 The date and details（日程と詳細）を主語に立てることで、文がわかりやすくなります。

05 us（われわれ）ではわかりにくいので、具体的な連絡（問い合わせ）先を記入したほうが明確です。

　［例］　**Human Resources**（人事部）

06 「ご協力ありがとうございます」は、通常 Thank you for your cooperation. とします。

添削反映バージョン

Information regarding email management seminar in April

The next email management seminar in April has been postponed because there weren't enough applicants.

We are sorry for the inconvenience.

Applicants who have already paid for the seminar will receive a refund. The next seminar will be scheduled in June. The date and details will be posted as soon as a decision is made.

Please contact Human Resources if you have any questions.

Thank you for your cooperation and understanding.

Miki Morita

> 同テーマで講師が書き下ろしたバージョン

April Email Management Seminar

The email management seminar scheduled for April has been postponed due to lack of applicants.

We apologize to those inconvenienced.

Applicants who have already made payment will receive a refund forthwith. The next seminar is scheduled for June. The date and details will be posted as soon as final decisions are made.

Please contact Human Resources if you have any questions.

Thank you for your cooperation and understanding.

Miki Morita

「同テーマで講師が書き下ろしたバージョン」語注

☐ **those inconvenienced**「これらの迷惑した（迷惑をかけた）人びと」
　those inconvenienced は、those (who were) inconvenienced の who were の部分を省略したものです。簡潔な文章にするため、以下のようにたびたびこういった省略が使われます。

［例］ **Those (who were) affected by the train delay had to take a bus.**
　　　電車の遅れで影響を受けた人びとはバスを使わなければならなかった。

☐ **forthwith**（副詞）「すぐさま」
　forthwith は、確定した日付は持たないが、「急いで準備します」ということをフォーマルに伝える状況（企業の公示、公表）でよく用いられます。

［例］ **The company acknowledges the battery problem and changes are coming forthwith.**
　　　その会社は、電源の問題を認め、すぐさま変更がなされることを公表した。

ビジネス文書 ④

英文履歴書

[メンバー情報]
M.O. 様／フリーランス／28 歳

[文の説明]
友人に頼まれてその履歴書を作成してみました。

原文

---

01. Taro Hashishita
02. taro@xxxxxx.jp

---

03. Education:
04. 1990
05. Graduated ABC University
06. BA in English literature

---

07. Related Work Experience:

---

08. May 2005 - May 2011

---

09. Work as a freelance Translator at home.

---

10. Translate business documents from English to Japanese including contracts, patents and computer operation manuals.

---

11. Oct 1995 - May 2005

12. AAA Co. Ltd.
13. Translator
14. Translate computer manuals from English to Japanese and translate Japanese emails into English.

---

15. Apr 1990 - Oct 1995

---

16. AAA English School
17. English Instructor
18. Student training / School correspondence / Teaching kids

---

19. Qualification
20. TOEIC 900

✏️ 添削

01. Taro Hashishita
02. taro@xxxxxx.jp

---

03. Education:
04. 1990
05. Graduated from ABC University
06. BA in English literature

---

07. Related Work Experience:

---

08. May 2005 - May 2011

09. ~~Work~~ Worked as a freelance translator ~~at home~~ from home.

10. ~~Translate~~ Translated business documents ~~from English to Japanese including~~ such as contracts, patents and computer operation manuals from English to Japanese.

11. ~~Oct~~ October 1995 - May 2005

12. AAA Co. Ltd.
13. Translator
14. ~~Translate~~ Translated computer manuals from English to Japanese and translated Japanese emails into English.

15. ~~Apr~~ April 1990 – ~~Oct~~ October 1995

16. AAA English School
17. English Instructor
18. Student training / School correspondence / Teaching kids

19. ~~Qualification~~ Qualifications
20. TOEIC 900

👉 解説

05 「～を卒業する」は graduate from ～です。前置詞 from が必要です。そして履歴書では、原文のように、普通は主語 I を省略します。

09 過去の経歴を表記するときは、通常過去形を使います。以下、例文を示します。

［例1］ **Supported** consultants on American accounts.

アメリカの会計について、コンサルタントをサポート（していました）。

［例2］ **Created** and **published** a marketing guide for the US market.

アメリカのマーケットに向けて、マーケティングガイドを作成および出版（していました）。

Eigobin Pointers 過去から現在の経歴を記すときには、一般的に現在進行形を使います。

以下、例文を示します。

［例3］ **2008 – Present: Working as a graphic designer.**

2008年から現在まで、グラフィックデザイナーとして働いています。

Eigobin Pointers フリーランスの翻訳者であれば、自宅で仕事することが予測されるため、at home は省略することもできます。また、「在宅で働く」という情報が必要なときは、work at home より、work from home とするほうがより一般的です。

以下、例文を示します。

［例4］ **Working from home** as an editor.

編集者として在宅で仕事をしています。

10 具体的な例をいくつか列挙する場合は、including（〜を含む）よりも、such as 〜（たとえば〜など）を使うほうが一般的です。また、business documents の具体例については、business documents such as 〜と直後に持ってきたほうがわかりやすく、文法的にも無理がありません。

11 履歴書では、日付は Apr, Oct のような略式ではなく、April, October のように省略せずに表記します。

19 たとえ1つの資格しか所有していない場合でも、Qualifications と複数形で記載します。

20 講師が書き下ろしたバージョンに追加したように、Microsoft Office Specialist Certification なども資格になります。

> 添削反映バージョン

Taro Hashishita
taro@xxxxxx.jp

Education:
1990
Graduated from ABC University
BA in English literature

Related Work Experience:

May 2005 - May 2011

Worked as a freelance translator from home.

Translated business documents such as contracts, patents and computer operation manuals from English to Japanese.

October 1995 - May 2005

AAA Co. Ltd.

Translator
Translated computer manuals from English to Japanese and translated Japanese emails into English.

April 1990 - October 1995

AAA English School
English Instructor
Student training / School correspondence / Teaching kids

Qualifications
TOEIC 900

> 同テーマで講師が書き下ろしたバージョン

Taro Hashishita

404 7-6-12 Yado
Yanoki City
Chiba 〒 690-3389
080-555-7171
Email: taro@xxxxxx.jp

Education

ABC University, Tokyo, Japan
— Bachelor of Arts degree with a major in English literature and

a minor in Philosophy
— Graduated with honors

Skills

— Self motivated with a high level of energy
— Excellent verbal communication skills
— Tolerant and flexible in different situations

Work Experience

Freelance Translator　　　　　　　　May 2005 – May 2011
— Translated a variety of business related documents such as contracts, patent requests, instruction manuals, and annual reports from English to Japanese
— Provided document revision service for material translated from Japanese to English

AAA Computer Co. Ltd.　　　　　October 1995 – May 2005

Translator/Editor
— Translated technical computer documents such as user manuals, maintenance manuals, and product specifications from English to Japanese
— Edited a variety of computer related documents translated by junior staff

AAA English School　　　　　　　April 1990 – October 1995

English Instructor
— Taught ESL to a wide variety of students including learners of

> all levels and ages
> — Developed courses for test preparation (TOEIC, TOEFL, STEP)
> — Generated original material for school textbook
>
> Qualifications
>
> TOEIC 900, Microsoft Office Specialist Certification (MOS)

「同テーマで講師が書き下ろしたバージョン」語注

☐ **graduate with honors**「大学の学部を優秀な成績で卒業する」
　[例]　**I'm hoping to graduate with honors. It all depends on my final exams.**
　　　優秀な成績で卒業したいと思っている。すべて卒業試験の結果次第だ。

☐ **self motivated**（形容詞）「自発的な」　ハイフンはあってもなくてもかまいません。
　[例]　**You really have to be self-motivated if you want to get ahead.**
　　　出世したいと思うなら、ほんとうに自発的でなければならない。

ビジネス文書 ⑤

操作マニュアル

[メンバー情報]
R.N. 様／専門職／30歳

[文の説明]
複合機におけるスキャニングの操作手順です。

原文

---

01. How to scan documents with multifunction device (MFD)

02. (1) Place the document to be scanned in the MFD.

03. (2) Touch your security card on the card reader.

04. (3) After performing authentication, select "Scan" button on the screen.

05. (4) Select the folder to save the scanned document in.

06. (5) Specify the settings including color scanning, two sided scanning and the number of copies.

07. (6) If you want to improve the scanning resolution, change the resolution on the "Layout Adjustment" tab.

08. (7) Press the "Start" button on the MFD.

✍🏻 添削

01. How to scan documents with multifunction device (MFD)

02. (1) Place the document to be scanned in the MFD.

03. (2) Touch your security card ~~on~~ to the card reader.

04. (3) After ~~performing~~ authentication, select the "Scan" button on the screen.

05. (4) Select the folder to save the scanned document in.

06. (5) Specify the settings including color scanning, two sided scanning and the number of copies.

07. (6) ~~If you want to improve the scanning resolution, change the resolution on the "Layout Adjustment" tab.~~ Enhance the scanning resolution with the "Layout Adjustment" tab if desired.

08. (7) Press the "Start" button on the MFD.

👉 解説

03 Touch your security card on the card reader. で意味は伝わるのですが、動詞 touch と 前置詞 on はあまり相性のいい組み合わせではありません。

以下のようにすると、より自然な英語になります。

[例1] **Place** your security card **on** the card reader.
セキュリティカードをカードリーダーの上に載せてください。

Eigobin Pointers リーダーの上にカードを載せるイメージが伝わります。

[例2] **Touch** your security card **to** the card reader.
セキュリティカードをカードリーダーに当ててください。

Eigobin Pointers セキュリティカードをリーダーに当ててタッチするイメージが伝わります。

[例3] **Touch** the card reader **with** your security card.
セキュリティカードでカードリーダーに触れてください。

Eigobin Pointers リーダーの場所にかかわらず、汎用的に使える表現です。

04 After performing authentication という表現自体に問題はないのですが、1つ前のステップで、セキュリティカードをリーダーに当てるという説明が入ってしまっているため、perform という動詞が使われると、何か別の動作が必要なのかと読み手に思われてしまう可能性があります。
　ここでは、新しい動作を起こさずに「カードが認証されるまで待つ」という意味が正確に伝わる文に修正しないといけません。
　以下、例文を示します。

[例1] **After being authorized,** select the "Scan" button on the screen.
[例2] **After authentication,** select the "Scan" button on the screen.

　特定の Scan ボタンを選択するので、定冠詞 the を付けて the Scan button とする必要があります。button を付けない場合は、"Scan" が固有名詞のような働きをするため、Select "Scan" on the screen. と定冠詞な

しで記述することが可能です。

07 前のステップまで命令形で書かれていますが、ここで If you want 〜と急に文スタイルが変わっています。全体の統一感を出すため、以下のような命令形に修正します。

[例1] **Enhance** the scanning resolution with the "Layout Adjustment" tab if desired.

[例2] **Change** the resolution by choosing the "Layout Adjustment" tab and making the changes.

添削反映バージョン

How to scan documents with a multifunction device (MFD)

(1) Place the document to be scanned in the MFD.

(2) Touch your security card to the card reader.

(3) After authentication, select the "Scan" button on the screen.

(4) Select the folder to save the scanned document in.

(5) Specify the settings including color scanning, two sided scanning and the number of copies.

(6) Enhance the scanning resolution with the "Layout Adjust-

ment" tab if desired.

(7) Press the "Start" button on the MFD.

> 同テーマで講師が書き下ろしたバージョン

How to scan documents with multifunction device (MFD)

(1) Place the document in the MFD.

(2) Place your security card on the card reader.

(3) After authorization, select "Scan" on the top screen.

(4) Select the folder the scanned document is to be saved in.

(5) Specify settings such as color scanning, two sided scanning and multiple copies if desired.

(6) Enhance the scanning resolution with the "Layout Adjustment" tab if desired.

(7) Press "Start".

「同テーマで講師が書き下ろしたバージョン」語注

☐ **if desired**「必要なら、ご希望でしたら」

［例］ **If desired, consumers can update the software at our website.**
必要であれば、お客様は私たちのサイトでソフトウェアをアップデートできる。

ビジネス文書 ⑥

ミーティングのお知らせ

[メンバー情報]
F.E. 様／営業職／32 歳

[文の説明]
次期経営管理システム設計について、社内打ち合わせの連絡です。

原文

01. A meeting to discuss the new management system for next year will be held on May 5 at the West 303 room.

02. The meeting will start at 1:00 pm and continue until the all the agenda will be discussed, so it's likely to take all afternoon.

03. All engineers and managers relating to develop the system need to attend. The department managers who are likely to use the system are expected to attend to collect all of the requirements from the user's point of view.

04. You need to have your proposal ready for the meeting.

05. Agenda:
06. 1. Purpose of the project
07. 2. Problem with the current system
08. 3. Improvements
09. 4. Schedule for the developments

10. If you can't attend the meeting, send your proposal via email to Takao Nagata by May 4.

✍ 添削

01. A meeting to discuss the new management system for next year will be held on May ~~5~~ 5th ~~at the~~ in West 303 ~~room~~.

02. The meeting will start at 1:00 pm and continue until ~~the~~ all of the agenda ~~will be~~ has been discussed~~, so~~. So it's likely to take all afternoon.

03. All engineers and managers ~~relating to~~ involved with ~~develop~~ developing the system need to attend. The department managers who are likely to use the system are expected to attend to collect all of the requirements from the user's point of view.

04. You need to have your proposal ready for the meeting.

05. Agenda:
06. 1. Purpose of the project
07. 2. ~~Problem~~ Problems with the current system
08. 3. Improvements
09. 4. Schedule for the developments

10. If you can't attend the meeting, send your proposal via email

to Takao Nagata by May ~~4~~ 4th.

👉 解説

01　社内の打ち合わせなどでは、May 5 という簡略な書き方も実際使われていますが、日付は 1st, 3rd, 5th と表記すると、「仕事ができる」という印象を与えます。

「～会議室で」と言うときは、in ～と前置詞 in を使います。

room（部屋、室）は、実際の名前の一部でない限り、書く必要はありません。

02　文が長すぎるので、「ミーティングの時間」と、「午後いっぱいかかる」の 2 つの文に分割します。

the all ～は、正しい英語表現ではありません。「すべての～」と言いたいときは、all ～（例：all books）、または all of the ～（例：all of the books）のどちらかを使います。

Eigobin Pointers　all of the ～の of は省略して、all the books とすることもできます。

時制が未来であっても、until（同様に when, while, before, after, as soon as）と will を、until ～ will ～のように同時に使うことはできません。通常、現在形か、現在完了形を使います。

　［例 1］　**Can you wait at the station until I come back?**（現在形）
　［例 2］　**Can you wait at the station until I've come back?**（現在完了形）
　　　　　私が戻ってくるまで駅で待っていていただけますか？

03　relate to ～には「～に関連している、～にかかわる」という意味があ

りますが、人間が主語になるときは、普通は「～とうまくかかわる」という人間的な関係を意味します。All engineers and managers relating to developing the system という文では、目的語が「開発すること」であり、人間的な関係がないために、不自然に聞こえます。ここでは involved with ～（～と関連を持つ）という表現が適しています。

以下、relate to を使った例文を示します。

[例]　**I'm always on time so I can't relate to people who are always late.**
私はいつも時間通りである。いつも遅れてくる人とはうまく付き合えない。

「システムの開発（をすること）」は、developing system または、system development のどちらかにすれば OK です。

07　「問題」は1つ以上あると思われるので、problems と複数形を使います。

＞ 添削反映バージョン

A meeting to discuss the new management system for next year will be held on May 5th in West 303.

The meeting will start at 1:00 pm and continue until all of the agenda has been discussed. So it's likely to take all afternoon.

All engineers and managers involved with developing the system need to attend. The department managers who are likely to use the system are expected to attend to collect all of the requirements from the user's point of view.

You need to have your proposal ready for the meeting.

Agenda:
1. Purpose of the project
2. Problems with the current system
3. Improvements
4. Schedule for the developments

If you can't attend the meeting, send your proposal via email to Takao Nagata by May 4th.

> 同テーマで講師が書き下ろしたバージョン

A meeting to discuss the new management system will be held on May 5th in West 303.

The meeting will start at 1:00 pm and continue all afternoon.

All engineers and managers involved with the development of the system are required to attend. Department managers whose departments will use the system are expected to attend to provide input and feedback on user needs.

Agenda:
1. Purpose of the project

> 2. Problems with the current system
> 3. Improvements
> 4. Schedule for development
>
> Please email Takao Nagata by May 4th at the latest if unable to attend.

「同テーマで講師が書き下ろしたバージョン」語注

□ **unable to** ～「～することができない」

　unable to attend（出席することができない）は、フォーマルな場面でていねいに誘いを断るときに使われる表現です。

　　［例］　**I'm afraid I am unable to attend because I have a previous engagement.**
　　　　　申し訳ございませんが、先の予定が入っており、出席することができません。

🏠 プライベートメール ①

プレゼントのお礼

[メンバー情報]
英語便 HN：milklove 様／主婦

[文の説明]
クリスマスプレゼントのお礼のメールです。

✏️ 原文

01. Dear Jack and Jackie,

02. How have you been?

03. How is the weather these days?

04. It's quite hot, isn't it? I hope you are staying cool.

05. It's strange to imagine the heat because it's winter here in Japan.

06. Thank you so much for the Christmas present!

07. I was really surprised, but very happy.

08. This is the first present I ever got from overseas.

09. So, my heart beat faster when I opened it.

10. It's really cute teddy bear I've wanted for a long time !

11. I can't find any words to thank you very much!

12. I'll keep it forever.

13. I hope you and your family are well this Christmas.

14. ... and, best wishes for the coming year.

15. Sincerely yours,

16. Kei

✍ 添削

01. Dear Jack and Jackie,

02. How have you been?

03. How is the weather in Australia these days?

04. It's quite hot, isn't it? I hope you are staying cool.

05. It's strange to imagine the heat because it's winter here in Japan.

06. Thank you so much for the Christmas present!

07. I was really surprised, ~~but~~ and very happy.

08. This is the first present I have ever got from overseas~~.~~

09. ~~So,~~ so my heart beat faster when I opened it.

10. It's ~~the~~ really cute teddy bear I've wanted for a long time!

11. I can't find ~~any~~ the words to thank you ~~very much~~ enough!

12. I'll keep it forever.

13. I hope you and your family ~~are well this~~ have a good Christmas.

14. ...and, best wishes for the coming year.

15. Sincerely yours,

16. Kei

解説

03 How is the weather these days?（最近の天気はどうですか？）は英語として正しいですが、読み手が遠くに住んでいるような場合は、in Australia のように相手のいる地域を加えることで、「そちらの天気はどうですか？」と気づかいを示すことができます。

07 ここでは、「ほんとうに驚いたけれど、すごくうれしい」と「けれど」

という「逆説」の表現が使われていることで、接続詞 but をあてたと思われます。ところが、I was really surprised（ほんとうに驚いた）という気持ちは、直前の文より、うれしい驚きのはずです。I was really surprised.（ほんとうに驚いた）と I am very happy.（ほんとうにうれしい）は両方ともうれしい気持ちを表わしているため、逆説 but でつなぐと、おかしなふうに聞こえてしまいます。ここでは and を使って文をつなげば、自然な文になります。

08 This is the first present I ever got from overseas. という文は、「これは、かつて私が海外から受け取った最初のプレゼントです」と、過去の出来事を語っているように聞こえます。今回は、現在の喜びを伝えるために、This is the first present I have ever got from overseas. と、現在完了形にします。現在完了を使うことで、今回のプレゼントは、「（過去から今までで）、はじめて海外から受け取ったもの」というニュアンスが伝わります。

09 so my heart beat faster when I opened it という部分は、直前の文と内容がつながっているため、文を分ける必要はありません。

10 ここで話しているテディベアは、自分が長いあいだほしがっていたものであり、この製品については前から知っていました。このため、ここでは定冠詞を使って、the really cute teddy bear とするのが適当です。

11 「お礼の言いようがありません」と言いたいときは、以下のような決まり文句で表現することができます。

[例1] **I can't find the words to thank you enough.**
　　　ことばにできないほど（ことばで言い尽くせないほど）感謝しています。

また、決まり文句ではありませんが、「ことばにならない」と言うときには、以下のような表現も利用可能です。

[例2]　**I can't find any words to express how happy I am!**
　　　うれしくて、ことばが見つかりません。

13　I hope you and your family are well this Christmas. という文は、this Christmas という期間を付け加えてしまったことで、「このクリスマスについては、あなたとご家族が元気でありますように」と、少しおかしな意味に聞こえます。（知人には、クリスマスだけではなく、ずっと元気でいてもらいたいはずです。）

　クリスマスの時期の挨拶であれば、以下のような文が適しています。

[例]　**I hope you and your family have a good Christmas.**
　　　あなたとご家族が、よいクリスマスを過ごされますように（よいクリスマスを）。

　　　　添削反映バージョン

Dear Jack and Jackie,

How have you been?
How is the weather in Australia these days?
It's quite hot, isn't it? I hope you are staying cool.
It's strange to imagine the heat because it's winter here in Japan.

Thank you so much for the Christmas present!
I was really surprised, and very happy.

This is the first present I have ever got from overseas, so my heart beat faster when I opened it.

It's the really cute teddy bear I've wanted for a long time!
I can't find the words to thank you enough!
I'll keep it forever.

I hope you and your family have a good Christmas.
...and, best wishes for the coming year.

Sincerely yours,

Kei

同テーマで講師が書き下ろしたバージョン

Dear Jack and Jackie,

How have you been?
How is the weather in Australia these days?
It's pretty hot I believe.
It's hard to imagine as it's winter here in Japan.

Thank you so much for the Christmas present!
I am so happy; you have no idea.

This is the first present I have ever had from overseas, so my heart was pounding when I opened it.

> It's the same really cute teddy bear I've wanted for ages.
> I can't find the words to thank you enough. I'll keep it forever.
>
> Have a wonderful Christmas and all the best for New Year.
>
> Regards,
>
> Kei

「同テーマで講師が書き下ろしたバージョン」語注

□ **hard to imagine**「考えられない」
　[例]　It's **hard to imagine** Dave ever being married.
　　　　デイヴがかつて結婚していたとは考えられない。

□ **you have no idea**「あなたにはわからない」
　you have no idea は、文字通りには「あなたにはわからない」という意味ですが、講師の例文のように、信じられないようなうれしい気持ちを伝える場面でもよく使われます。
　講師のセンテンスは、you have no idea (how happy I am) の how happy I am「私がどんなにうれしいか」の部分が省略されています。
　[例]　**You have no idea** how much I appreciate your patience.
　　　　私がどんなにあなたの辛抱強さに感謝しているか、あなたにはわからないと思います。(⇨あなたの辛抱強さにものすごく感謝しています。)

🏠 プライベートメール ②

誕生日のお祝い

[メンバー情報]
C.Y. 様／技術職／34 歳

[文の説明]
友人のお子さんは、自分の息子より3ヶ月早く産まれました。その友だちの子供に送る1歳の誕生日のお祝いメールです。

✏️ 原文

---

01. Happy First Birthday Ken.

02. I hope the following year will be another wonderful one.

03. 1 year ago I met you for the first time. You were very tiny and only sleep or cry.

04. Every time I saw you, you could do new things. Now you can walk and say a few words.

05. It is amazing how much you have grown up.

06. You are 3 months older than my son so I imagine my son doing 3 months follow.

07. I am glad that you play with my son. Please be nice to my son from this.

08. I heard you like picture books very much and you often beg for your mother to read them.

09. I give you picture books for your birthday. I hope you like them.

10. Lots of love,

11. Hirochi

✍ 添削

01. Happy First Birthday Ken.

02. I hope the following year will be another wonderful one.

03. ~~1~~ One year ago I met you for the first time. You were very tiny and only ~~sleep~~ slept or ~~cry~~ cried.

04. Every time I saw you, you could do new things. Now you can walk and say a few words.

05. It is amazing how much you have grown ~~up~~.

06. You are ~~3~~ three months older than my son so I imagine my son doing those things ~~3 three months follow~~ over the following three months.

07. I am glad that you play with my son. ~~Please be nice to my son from this.~~ Please continue to be nice to my son.

08. I heard you like picture books very much and you often beg ~~for~~ your mother to read them.

09. I ~~give~~ am giving you picture books for your birthday. I hope you like them.

10. Lots of love,

11. Hirochi

👉 解説

03 一桁の数字 (1〜9) を書くときには、一般的に 1, 2, 3 と数字そのままではなく、one, two, three 〜と spell out したほうがわかりやすくなります。特に、数字が文頭にくるときは、10 以上の数字でも、Eleven のような表記を一般的に使います。

　You were very tiny「あなたはとても小さかった」と過去のことを書いていますので、あとにつづく部分も only slept or cried（寝ているか泣いているだけだった）と過去形にします。

05　grow up は基本的に「大人になる」という意味ですので、赤ちゃんや幼児の成長を表現するのにはふさわしくありません。grow（成長する）だけでいいでしょう。

　以下、grow up の例文を示します。

　[例]　**Dave's son Jimmy really grew up after going to summer camp.**

デイヴの息子ジミーは、夏合宿へ行ったあと、ほんとうに大人になった。

06　my son doing だけでは、何をするのか意味があいまいです。目的語の those things を付け加えることで、前項の「歩いたり、話したりする」ことを指していることが明確になります。

　follow は「〜につづく」という意味の動詞、または「あとを追うこと」という意味の名詞であり、〜 months follow という言い方はできません。「その後 3 ヶ月にわたって」と言うときは、over the following three months とすればいいです。

Eigobin Pointers　ここでは、three months later「3 ヶ月後」, three months from now「今から 3 ヶ月」という表現もできます。

07　be nice to my son from this は、場合によっては、「（今まではやさしくなかったので）これからはやさしくしてくださいね」というふうに聞こえてしまいます。

　「今までも、そしてこれからもずっとうちの息子にやさしくしてね」と言うときは、Please continue to be nice to my son. とすればいいでしょう。

08　beg「せがむ」は「beg + 人」、または、「beg for + 物」のいずれかで表現します。以下、例文を示します。

　［例 1］　**I used to beg my mother to take me to work with her.**
　　　　　私はよく母親に、仕事に一緒に連れていってくれとせがみました。

　［例 2］　**Kids usually have to beg for their allowance.**
　　　　　子供たちは、通常小遣いをせがむものである。

09　「（誕生日の）プレゼントを贈ります」と言う場合、以下のような表現がよく使われます。

　［例 1］　**I'm giving you picture books.**

絵本を贈ります。

[例2] **I bought (got) you picture books.**

絵本をあなたのために買い求めました。

> 添削反映バージョン

Happy First Birthday Ken.

I hope the following year will be another wonderful one.

One year ago I met you for the first time. You were very tiny and only slept or cried.
Every time I saw you, you could do new things. Now you can walk and say a few words.

It is amazing how much you have grown.

You are three months older than my son so I imagine my son doing those things over the following three months.
I am glad that you play with my son. Please continue to be nice to my son.

I heard you like picture books very much and you often beg your mother to read them.
I am giving you picture books for your birthday. I hope you like them.

Lots of love,

Hirochi

> 同テーマで講師が書き下ろしたバージョン

Happy First Birthday Ken.

I hope the following year will be another wonderful one.

I met you for the first time, just one year ago today. You were so tiny, and only slept or cried. Every time I saw you, you could do something new. Now you can walk, and say a few words.

It's amazing how much you've grown.

You are three months older than my son, so when I look at you I think my son will do those things when he's your age.

I'm so happy you play together.

I heard you're into picture books very much and you beg your mother to read them to you, so I've given you a few for your birthday. I hope you like them!

Lots of love,

Hirochi

「同テーマで講師が書き下ろしたバージョン」語注

□ **Lots of love**「たくさんの愛を込めて」

　Love または Lots of love は手紙やメールの最後によく書かれる、家族や親しい友人など、おもに近しい相手に対して使われる挨拶です。

　日本語で「愛を込めて」と言っても、英語では日常の挨拶に近く、Lots of love, Hugs and kissing, All my love などの挨拶は男性同士でもよく書きます。

　また、Love to all（家族のみんなへ）という挨拶も一般的です。

🏠 プライベートメール ③

旅行に誘う

[メンバー情報]
K.K. 様／主婦／47 歳

[文の説明]
友人を別荘に招待するメールです。

✏️ 原文

01. Hello Perri,

02. How have you been? I hope you are well.

03. Summer has come. My children are enjoying their summer vacation.

04. They make me busier than usual, but we are really enjoying ourselves playing in the little swimming pool in my garden, go shopping, and studying homework every day.

05. I heard you and your family are staying your parents' house this summer.

06. I'm sure that all of you must be having a good time together.

07. As you know, we are going to go to Aso in Kumamoto next weekend. My parents have a second house there. We are going to stay there for two or three days.

08. Why don't you come with us? We haven't seen each other for a long time.
I would really like to see all of you!

09. It takes about an hour and a half from my house.
If you go there, you can take JR from Kumamoto to Aso Station, then I will pick you up and take you to our place by my car.

10. There are many places to visit around the house, not only Mt. Aso but also a big resort facility which was built next to the house last year. There are many good restaurants and hot springs there.

11. If you have interest in this plan, send me an e-mail before Wednesday, and let's make arrangements together. It is the best season to visit Aso!

12. It would be nice for us to see each other and enjoy our summer vacation together.

13. Love,

14. Keiko

✍️ 添削

01. Hello Perri,

02. How have you been? I hope you are well.

03. Summer has come. My children are enjoying their summer vacation.

04. They make me busier than usual, but we are really enjoying ourselves playing in the little swimming pool in my garden, ~~go~~ going shopping, and ~~studying~~ doing homework every day.

05. I heard you and your family are staying at your parents' house this summer.

06. I'm sure that all of you must be having a good time together.

07. As you know, we are going to go to Aso in Kumamoto next weekend. My parents have a second house there. We are going to stay there for two or three days.

08. ~~Why don't you come with us?~~ Why don't you come and visit us at that time? We haven't seen each other for a long time. I would really like to see all of you!

09. It takes about an hour and a half from my house. If you ~~go~~ come ~~there~~, you can take JR from Kumamoto to Aso Station, then I will pick you up and take you to our place by ~~my~~ car.

10. There are many places to visit around the house, not only Mt. Aso but also a big resort facility which was built ~~next to~~ near the house last year. There are many good restaurants and hot springs there.

11. If you ~~have interest in this plan~~ would like to come, send me an e-mail before Wednesday, and let's make arrangements together. It is the best season to visit Aso!

12. It would be nice for us to see each other and enjoy our summer vacation together.

13. Love,

14. Keiko

👉 解説

04 ここでは、「庭のプールで遊ぶ」「買い物に行く」「宿題をする」という3つの行為を並べて記述しています。はじめの「プールで泳ぐ」を playing in the little swimming pool と進行形ではじめていますので、文のスタイルを揃えるために、後続の2つも going shopping（買い物に行く），doing homework（宿題をする）と進行形にします。

「宿題をする」と言う場合は、動詞は study ではなく、do を使い、do homework とします。

以下、例文を示します。

[例] **Doing homework** isn't usually a child's favorite activity.

宿題は普通、子供が喜んでするものではない。

05 「〜へ滞在する」と言うときは、stay at 〜 と前置詞 at が必要です。
以下、例文を示します。

　[例]　**I will stay at a hotel in Kyoto.**
　　　京都のホテルへ滞在します。

08　Why don't you come with us? は文法的に正しいのですが、友人と一緒に行って、一緒に帰る旅行のようなイメージを読み手に与えます。今回のように、滞在先に「遊びに来てもらいたい」「立ち寄ってもらいたい」と言うときには、通常 come and visit という表現を使います。
　以下、例文を示します。

　[例]　**You can come and visit us anytime.**
　　　いつでも私たちのところへ立ち寄ってください。

09　前項で、Why don't you come and visit us? と come を使っているため、go（行く）ではなく、同じ come（来る）を使ったほうが意味がわかりやすくなります。
　また、there（そこ）に来ることは明らかなので、ここでは省略することができます。
　「車で」は by car と所有格なしで記述します。
　以下、例文を示します。

　[例]　**It takes 50 minutes by car to Haneda airport.**
　　　羽田空港まで車で 50 分かかります。

10　next to 〜は「隣接して」という意味になります。ここでは、近くにできたリゾート施設についての記述と思われますので、near（近くにある）が適当です。

11 If you have interest in this plan(このプランに興味があれば)という言い方は、友人へのメールで使うには、フォーマルすぎて不自然です。別の言い方にしたほうがいいでしょう。以下、例文を示します。

[例1] **If you would like to come, email me by Wednesday.**
もし来たければ、水曜日までにメールをください。

[例2] **If you're interested, email me by Wednesday.**
もし興味があれば、水曜日までにメールをください。

添削反映バージョン

Hello Perri,

How have you been? I hope you are well.

Summer has come. My children are enjoying their summer vacation.
They make me busier than usual, but we are really enjoying ourselves playing in the little swimming pool in my garden, going shopping, and doing homework every day.

I heard you and your family are staying at your parents' house this summer.
I'm sure that all of you must be having a good time together.
As you know, we are going to go to Aso in Kumamoto next weekend. My parents have a second house there. We are going to stay there for two or three days.

Why don't you come and visit us at that time? We haven't seen each other for a long time. I would really like to see all of you!
It takes about an hour and a half from my house. If you come, you can take JR from Kumamoto to Aso Station, then I will pick you up and take you to our place by car.

There are many places to visit around the house, not only Mt. Aso but also a big resort facility which was built near the house last year. There are many good restaurants and hot springs there.

If you would like to come, send me an e-mail before Wednesday, and let's make arrangements together.
It is the best season to visit Aso!
It would be nice for us to see each other and enjoy our summer vacation together.

Love,

Keiko

> 同テーマで講師が書き下ろしたバージョン

Hello Perri,

How have you been? I hope you are well.

Summer has finally come! My children are enjoying their summer vacation.
I'm rushed off my feet more than usual, but we are really enjoying ourselves every day playing in the little swimming pool in my garden, going shopping, and doing their homework.

I heard you and your family are staying at your parents' house this summer.
I'm sure that all of you are having a fantastic time together.

By the way, we are off to Aso in Kumamoto for a few days next weekend.
My parents have a second house there, as you know.

Why don't you come and visit us at that time? We haven't seen each other for the longest time. I really would like to see you all!

It takes about an hour and a half from my house to get there. If you come, you can take the JR line from Kumamoto to Aso station, then I will pick you up.

There are many places to visit around the house, not only Mt. Aso but also a big resort that was built near the house last year. There are a bunch of restaurants and hot springs there.

If you would like to come, send me a mail before Wednesday, and let's try and fix something up. Now is the best time to visit Aso!

It would be nice for us to see each other and enjoy the summer vacation together.

Love,

Keiko

「同テーマで講師が書き下ろしたバージョン」語注

□ **be rushed off my feet**「仕事に追いまわされる、てんてこまいである」
［例］ **I** hate the end of the month because I'm always **rushed off my feet**.
月末は嫌いだ。いつも仕事に追いまわされる。

□ **be off to** 〜「〜へ出発する、出かける」
［例］ **I'm off to** Hakone this weekend to relax.
今週末、リラックスするために箱根へ出かける。

□ **for the longest time**「とても長いあいだ」
［例］ **I** haven't rented a DVD **for the longest time**.
ずい分長いあいだDVDを借りていない。

□ **fix up**（句動詞）「手はずを整える、手配する」
［例］ **I'm** not sure if she's available, but I'll try and **fix** something **up** for next weekend.
彼女が空いているかどうかはよくわからないけど、次週に手配してみます。

プライベートメール ④

誘いを断る

[メンバー情報]
河田　美紗子様／コーヒーメーカー営業／24歳

[文の説明]
キャンプに誘われましたが、忙しくて誘いを断るメールです。

原文

01. Hi Cathy,

02. Thank you for asking me to go to a camp this autumn.

03. It sounds great. I really wanted to go, but I've found I'm pretty busy towards September. I have to give up.

04. One of my colleagues broke her ankle, and was hospitalized this month, so I need to follow up all her work. I work till around 10:00 pm every day.

05. I have no idea when I can take a few days vacation.

06. I am so sorry to tell you at the last minute.

07. Let me join in next time. Say hello to everyone.

08. Bye,

09. Misako

✎ 添削

01. Hi Cathy,

02. Thank you for asking me to go ~~to a camp~~ camping this autumn.

03. It sounds great, and I really wanted to go, but ~~I've found I'm pretty busy towards~~ I'm going to be pretty busy in September. ~~I have to give up.~~ I'm sorry but I can't come.

04. One of my colleagues broke her ankle, and was hospitalized this month, so I need to follow up all her work. At the moment I ~~work~~ am working till around 10:00 pm every day.

05. I have no idea when I can take a few days vacation.

06. I am so sorry to tell you at the last minute.

07. Let me join in next time. Say hello to everyone.

08. Bye,

09. Misako

👉 解説

02 英語の a camp は、通常、たとえば合宿のような「特別の目的があり、管理された環境のなかで過ごす活動」を指します。

［例］ **a baseball camp**
　　　野球合宿

テントを張って、バーベキューを楽しむようなキャンプの場合は、camping を使って、go camping（キャンプに行く）とするのがいいでしょう。

03　この場合、2つの文が内容的につながりがあるので、and を使って1つの文にするのがいいと思います。

　I've found 〜という表現は、一定期間をかけて何かを発見したようなときに使われます。今回は、キャンプの誘いを受けて、スケジュール上無理だという事実を伝えているので（特に一定期間考えて気づいたことではないため）、I've found と書きはじめると不自然な表現になってしまいます。ここでは、I'm going to be pretty busy in September.（9月はものすごく忙しくなる予定）と未来形で表現することで、自然な英語になります。

　I've found を使った文例を以下に示します。

［例１］　**I've found this new application has saved me a lot of time.**
　　　　　この新しいアプリケーションを使うと、かなり時間が節約できることがわかった。

　一定期間、あるアプリケーションを使っているうちに、時間が節約できることに気づいたので、I've found を使って表現するのが自然です。

　日本語では「今回は行くのをあきらめる」と言える場面ですが、英語の give up は通常「すでに何かをはじめているものを、途中であきらめる」ときに使われます。

自分で計画していたキャンプをあきらめるのではなく、誘いが来た時点で忙しくて行けないという状況では give up を使うよりも、I'm sorry but I can't come.（ごめんなさい。行けそうもありません）という表現が適しています。
　give up を使った文例を以下に示します。

［例2］　**I gave up half way up Mt. Fuji because it was too difficult.**
あまりに大変で、富士山の中腹であきらめました。

04　I need to follow up all her work. は、以下のようにすることも可能です。

［例1］　**I need to cover all her work.**
すべての彼女の仕事を代替する必要がある。

［例2］　**I need to do all her work.**
すべての彼女の仕事をやる必要がある。

　I work till around 10:00 pm every day. と現在形で記述すると、通常いつも10時まで働いているように聞こえます。今だけ、同僚の怪我のために遅くまで働いているということであれば、at the moment（現時点では）と追記し、I am working till around 10:00 pm every day. と現在進行形を使うことによって、「現時点ではこうしている」という意味が伝わります。

添削反映バージョン

Hi Cathy,

Thank you for asking me to go camping this autumn.

It sounds great, and I really wanted to go, but I'm going to be pretty busy in September. I'm sorry but I can't come.
One of my colleagues broke her ankle, and was hospitalized this month, so I need to follow up all her work. At the moment I am working till around 10:00 pm every day.

I have no idea when I can take a few days vacation.
I am so sorry to tell you at the last minute.

Let me join in next time. Say hello to everyone.

Bye,

Misako

同テーマで講師が書き下ろしたバージョン

Hi Cathy,

Thank you for inviting me to go on your camping trip.

It sounds great and I would really like to go but I'm extremely busy at the moment. One of my colleagues has broken her ankle and I have to cover for her at work. For the time being I'll be working till around 10:00 pm every day. I have no idea when I can next take a few days off.

Please say hello to everyone from me. I hope to be able to join you all on a camping trip sometime in the future.

Bye,

Misako

「同テーマで講師が書き下ろしたバージョン」語注

□ **for the time being**「さしあたり、当分のあいだ」

[例] **Jim is going to keep his job for the time being.**
ジムはしばらくのあいだ仕事をつづけるつもりだ。

「さしあたり、当分のあいだ」という意味では、for a while も同様に使われます。

🏠 プライベートメール ⑤

感動を伝える

[メンバー情報]
英語便HN：yumiyumayume 様／チャイナペインター／46歳

[文の説明]
妊娠中の私を気遣う母に、クラシックコンサートの報告をするメールです。

✏️ **原文**

01. Hi, Mom. How have you been? As you know, I went to a classic concert with Seiji. You really don't need to worry about me because I am quite fine. I really enjoyed the concert with him and our baby.

02. Actually, I never expected what happened to me, but...... I was so excited the concert. It was great! So, I guess our baby was also very excited, and she was moving in my stomach during the concert. I was glad that I could feel her closer, and I could share my feelings with her. It was my first time to feel that she was alive, and she also could hear music. I was very inspired by the moment when she turned over. She did it a lot when the concert became terrific! I really think that she can understand classic music.

03. What did you feel when I moved in you? Were you really looking forward to seeing me in person? I am really looking forward to seeing her in person right now. I have to appreciate the concert because it let me realize that I would be-

come a mom three months from now. I am still not confident in becoming a good mom, but I would like to try my best, Mom!

04. I think that I can sleep well tonight. When I told the story that our baby moved a lot in me, Seiji seemed to be so happy. I am glad to know that he is also looking forward to seeing her in person. I can tell you that he will become a good dad! I am sure today's concert is the best because I am eaten up with love.

05. Meanwhile, say hello to dad. Nighty night.

06. Your daughter, Yumi with love

添削

01. Hi, Mom. How have you been? As you know, I went to a ~~classic~~ classical concert with Seiji. You really don't need to worry about me because I am quite fine. I really enjoyed the concert with him and our baby.

02. Actually, I never expected what happened to me, but...... I was so excited by the concert. It was great! So, I guess our baby was also very excited, and she was moving ~~in~~ inside ~~my stomach~~ me during the concert. I was glad that I could feel ~~her~~ closer to her, and I could share my feelings with her.

It was my first time to feel that she was alive~~, and~~ because she also could hear the music. I was very inspired by the ~~moment~~ moments when she turned ~~over~~. She did it a lot when the concert became terrific! I really think that she can understand ~~classic~~ classical music.

---

03. What did you feel when I moved in you? Were you really looking forward to seeing me in person? I am really looking forward to seeing her ~~in person~~ right now. I ~~have to appreciate~~ am grateful for the concert because it let me realize that I would become a mom three months from now. I am still not confident in becoming a good mom, but I would like to try my best, Mom!

---

04. I think that I can sleep well tonight. When I told the story ~~that~~ about how our baby moved a lot in me, Seiji seemed to be so happy. I am glad to know that he is also looking forward to seeing her in person. I can tell you that he will become a good dad! I am sure today's concert is the best I have ever been to because I am eaten up with love.

---

05. Meanwhile, say hello to dad. Nighty night.

---

06. Your daughter, Yumi with love

👉 解説

01 日本でいう「クラシック音楽」のジャンルは、英語では classical music と言います。classic music という表現は、音楽のジャンルではな

く、長年を経てもいまだに人気のある音楽に対して使われます。たとえば、ビートルズの "Let It Be" やビーチボーイズの "Don't Worry Baby" は、classic song（往年の名曲）と言えるでしょう。

02 「～に興奮する、わくわくする」と言うときは、be excited by［at］～と前置詞が必要です。

Eigobin Pointers I was excited at the concert. と前置詞に at を用いると、「コンサートで聞いている音楽に胸を躍らせました」と読み手が「音楽」がよかったと想像します。

　stomach は広義で「腹部」という意味があり、このような文脈でよく用いられますが、厳密には子宮は stomach に含まれないので、inside me と表現するのがいいでしょう。

　「心理的に～に近い（より近い）」は、feel close (closer) to ～とすればいいと思います。

　she also could hear the music（彼女も音楽を聴くことができた）というのは、お腹の赤ちゃんが生きていると感じることができた理由であるため、接続詞 and よりも because を使ったほうが自然な文になります。

　ここでの music は、「このコンサートで演奏された特定の音楽」であるので、定冠詞の the が必要です。

　moment と単数形にすると、1回限りになりますが、赤ちゃんが何回も turned（動いた）のであれば、複数形の moments を使うべきです。

　turned over は「反転した、180度回転した」という意味になるので、赤ちゃんが動いたことを表現するのであれば、over は不要です。

03　2つ目の in person（直接、じかに）は、直前の文で使われていて明らかなので、ここでは省略できます。

　appreciate「～を感謝する」は、通常、I appreciate your help.（あなたの助けを感謝している）というように、通常は人が自分（自分たち）のためにしてくれたことに対して用います。ここでは、「コンサートでの経験に感謝している」という意味ですので、appreciate ではなく、be grateful for ～（～に感謝している）が適当です。

04 「～という話を伝える」と言いたいときは、構文としては tell the story that ～ ではなく、S tell (O) a story about ～か、もしくは S tell O that ～のどちらかを使うべきです。

例文を挙げて説明します。

[例1]　**She told me a story about going to Hawaii.**
　　　　彼女は私にハワイに言った話を伝えた。

[例2]　**She told me that she went to Hawaii.**
　　　　彼女は私にハワイに行ったことを伝えた。

When I told the story about how our baby moved a lot in me は、When I told Seiji that our baby moved a lot in me としても可能です。

「今まで行ったなかで最高の」という意味で、the best I have ever been to と修正します。

添削反映バージョン

Hi, Mom. How have you been? As you know, I went to a classical concert with Seiji. You really don't need to worry about me because I am quite fine. I really enjoyed the concert with him and our baby.

Actually, I never expected what happened to me, but...... I was so excited by the concert. It was great! So, I guess our baby was also very excited, and she was moving inside me during the concert. I was glad that I could feel closer to her, and I could share my feelings with her. It was my first time to feel that she was alive because she also could hear the music. I was very inspired by the moments when she turned. She did it a lot when the concert became terrific! I really think that she can understand classical music.

What did you feel when I moved in you? Were you really looking forward to seeing me in person? I am really looking forward to seeing her right now. I am grateful for the concert because it let me realize that I would become a mom three months from now. I am still not confident in becoming a good mom, but I would like to try my best, Mom!

I think that I can sleep well tonight. When I told the story about how our baby moved a lot in me, Seiji seemed to be so happy. I am glad to know that he is also looking forward to seeing her in person. I can tell you that he will become a good dad! I am sure today's concert is the best I have ever been to because I am eaten up with love.

Meanwhile, say hello to dad. Nighty night.

Your daughter, Yumi with love

同テーマで講師が書き下ろしたバージョン

Hi Mom,

How have you been? Going to the concert with Seiji was no problem. You really didn't have to worry about anything. The baby was fine and we had a great time.

Actually, I was quite surprised that I got so excited at the concert. It was incredible. The baby was also very excited. I could feel it kicking all through the concert. There were several moments when it seemed like she was kicking in time with the music. I thought it was one of those very special experiences between a mother and daughter.

Do you remember when I was a tiny baby inside you? I can finally imagine how it must have felt. The anticipation is overwhelming. Did you feel it too? I can hardly wait to see her in person. It's funny, the concert helped me fully realize that I'm going to be a mother in three months. I'm very nervous about it, but I'll do my best.

Seiji was very happy when I told him how much the baby moved during the concert. He's as excited as me about the baby coming. I'm sure he'll be a great dad.

Anyway, it was a great concert that I will never forget.

Love you,

> Yumi
>
> PS — Say hi to dad.

「同テーマで講師が書き下ろしたバージョン」語注

☐ **in time**「調子を合わせて」
　[例]　**I always walk in time with the music.**
　　　　私はいつも音楽に調子を合わせて歩いている。

☐ **one of those**「よくある」
　[例]　**He is one of those guys who always talks about himself.**
　　　　彼は、よくいる自分のことばかり話す人だ。

プライベートメール ⑥

友人を励ます

[メンバー情報]
楊　博美様／システムエンジニア／31歳

[文の説明]
足を骨折して、ホノルルマラソン出場をあきらめた友人を励ますメールです。

原文

01. Hi Jack,

02. It's Hiromi. I heard you broke your leg jogging, and you won't run the next Honolulu Marathon.

03. I know you were practicing very hard and how much you are frustrated now.

04. I think it's time to rest, eat something delicious, read something interesting, and watch your favorite movies.

05. I'm sure the good rest will bring you a good result in the future.

06. Anytime email me or call me when you need someone to talk to.

07. I hope you get well soon.

```
--------------------------------------------------
08. Hiromi
--------------------------------------------------
```

📝 添削

01. Hi Jack,

02. It's Hiromi. I heard you broke your leg jogging, ~~and~~ so you won't run the next Honolulu Marathon.

03. I know you were practicing very hard ~~and how much you are frustrated now.~~ You must be very frustrated now.

04. I think it's time to rest, eat something delicious, read something interesting, and watch your favorite movies.

05. I'm sure ~~the good rest will bring you a good result in the future~~ the rest will be good for you.

06. ~~Anytime email~~ Email ~~me~~ or call me anytime ~~when~~ if you need someone to talk to.

07. I hope you get well soon.

08. Hiromi

👉 解説

02 「足の骨折が原因で、ホノルルマラソンで走れなくなった」という原因と結果の関係になっているので、接続詞 and（〜と）より so（それで）で結ぶほうが自然な文になります。

分詞構文は、副詞句として、時、原因・理由、付帯状況、条件譲歩などの意味を表わします。I heard you broke your leg jogging. の文では、broke your leg「足を折った」＋付帯状況として、jogging（ジョギングする）で２つの動作が同時に行なわれたことが示されています。（jogging の部分が「ジョギングしながら」という意味になります。）

同じような分詞構文の付帯状況の例文を示します。

[例１]　**I was sitting on the sofa watching TV.**
テレビを見ながら、ソファーに座っていた。

付帯状況は、そのあとほかの出来事がつづけて起こる場合もあります。

[例２]　**A boy came up to me asking if I wanted to buy the puppets.**
１人の少年が私のところにやってきて、その人形が買いたいかどうか尋ねた。

03 「過去に熱心に練習していたこと」と、「現在骨折で悔しい思いをしていること」は別の事柄なので、２つの文に分割したほうがわかりやすくなります。

相手の気持ちを察するときは、You must be 〜 とすれば、それがあなたの「心からの気持ち」であると伝わります。以下、例文を示します。

[例１]　**You must be tired after such a long trip.**
長い旅行のあとで疲れているでしょう。

[例２]　**You must be relieved after seeing your test result.**
テストの結果を見て安心していることでしょう。

05 the good rest will bring you a good result in the future（いい休憩はいい結果をもたらす）だと、相手の体調についてのことなのか、次のレースについてのことなのか、はっきりしません。以下のどちらかの文にすることで、明確になります。

［例1］　**I'm sure the rest will be good for you.**
　　　　休むことは、あなたにとっていいことだと思いますよ。
Eigobin Pointers　相手の体調を気遣っていることが伝わります。

［例2］　**I'm sure the rest will help you do better in the next race.**
　　　　休むことで、次のレースでいい結果を残せると思いますよ。
Eigobin Pointers　「今は休んで、次のレースでがんばってほしい」という気持ちが伝わります。

06 anytime は通常、修飾するものの直後に置きます。ここでは email or call me（Eメールや電話をすること）の直後に置きます。
anytime を使った例文を示します。

［例］　**She told me that I could drop in anytime.**
　　　　彼女は、私にいつでも立ち寄るように言った。

Eigobin Pointers　anytime は drop in（立ち寄る）を修飾しています。
　email me or call me というのはやや冗長です。email or call me と、目的語を1つにまとめることができます。
　when you need ～は問題ないのですが、こういった場面では、「もし必要だったら～」という意味を出すため、if you need ～とするのがさらに適当です。

> 添削反映バージョン

Hi Jack,

It's Hiromi. I heard you broke your leg jogging, so you won't run the next Honolulu Marathon.
I know you were practicing very hard.
You must be very frustrated now.

I think it's time to rest, eat something delicious, read something interesting, and watch your favorite movies.

I'm sure the rest will be good for you.

Email or call me anytime if you need someone to talk to.

I hope you get well soon.

Hiromi

> 同テーマで講師が書き下ろしたバージョン

Hi Jack,

It's Hiromi. I heard you broke your leg jogging. I'm really sorry to hear that. Are you still in any pain?

It must be especially disappointing since you had been training so hard for the Honolulu Marathon. I really feel for you.

But anyway, please make sure you don't rush back into training before your leg has properly healed. Catch up on some movies, read some good books, hey, maybe you should even eat a few of those things you have been denying yourself recently. Now is your chance!

Email or call me anytime.

Looking forward to hearing from you.

Hiromi

「同テーマで講師が書き下ろしたバージョン」語注

□ **in pain**「痛くて」
   [例] **It's really hard to concentrate when you are in pain.**
   痛みのあるときに集中するのはむずかしい。

□ **feel for 〜**「〜に同情する」
   [例] **I really feel for all the people who have been effected by the recession.**
   その景気後退で影響を受けた人びとに、心から同情する。

□ **rush back**「慌てて戻る、大急ぎで戻る」

[例]　**If you aren't ready, you shouldn't rush back into it.**
準備ができていないなら、急いで戻るべきではない。

📖 ショートエッセイ

問題点をまとめる

[メンバー情報]
内田　貴弘様／部品メーカー営業／31歳

[文の説明]
職場で実際に起きている経験を元に、アウトソースにおける利点・問題点をまとめてみました。

📝 問題

Is Outsourcing Overseas Always a Good Idea?

✏️ 原文

01. I think outsourcing overseas is generally a good idea.

02. As globalization goes on, business cannot be competitive without global perspectives.

03. Outsourcing is one of the important keys to lower the labor cost. Companies often replace their support staff or software developers with outsourced workers.

04. It may just rise in the jobless rate in Japan, and help leaking internal technologies.

05. However, outsourcing creates new talents and opportunities

in other countries.

06. The balance between benefit and backlash should be always considered properly.

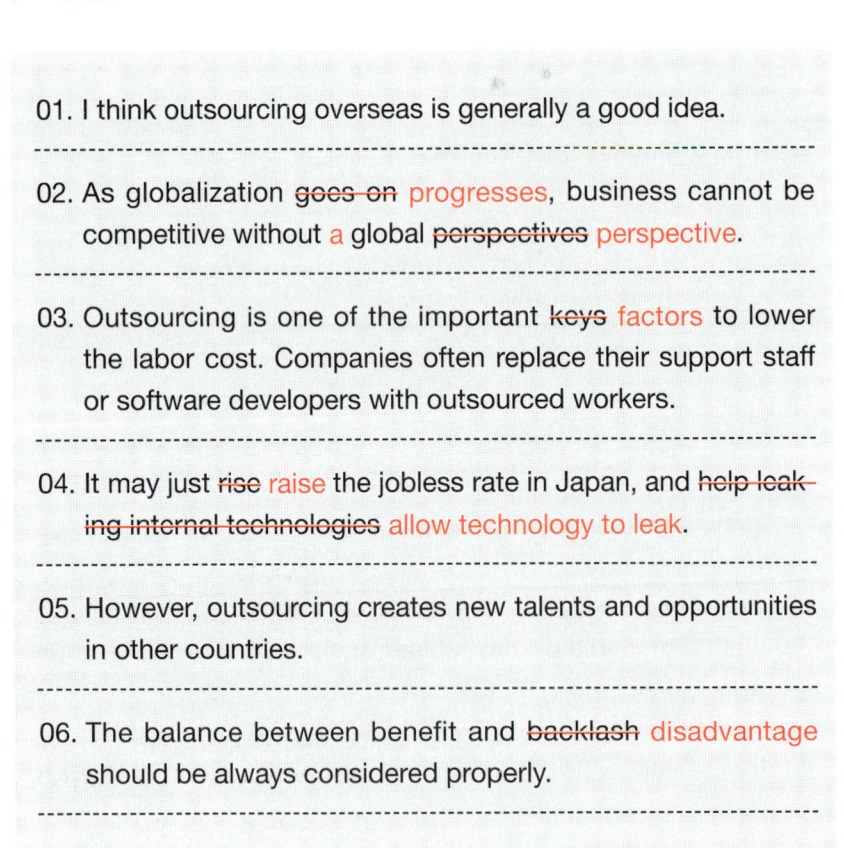

✎ 添削

01. I think outsourcing overseas is generally a good idea.

02. As globalization ~~goes on~~ progresses, business cannot be competitive without a global ~~perspectives~~ perspective.

03. Outsourcing is one of the important ~~keys~~ factors to lower the labor cost. Companies often replace their support staff or software developers with outsourced workers.

04. It may just ~~rise~~ raise the jobless rate in Japan, and ~~help leaking internal technologies~~ allow technology to leak.

05. However, outsourcing creates new talents and opportunities in other countries.

06. The balance between benefit and ~~backlash~~ disadvantage should be always considered properly.

👉 解説

02 go on（進みつづける）でも問題はありませんが、progress（前進する、進歩する）または expand（拡大する）のほうが、アカデミックライティングにふさわしい感じがします。

　global perspective（グローバルな視点）は、1つの視点なので単数表記にします。

03 単語 key には「重要な手がかり」という意味合いがあるため、important keys は意味の重なりを感じます。したがって、factor（要因）を使って、important factors と修正します。

04 「上昇する」という意味の rise は自動詞であり、目的語を持ちません。他動詞 raise（上昇させる）か、increase（増加させる）を使います。
　以下、rise と raise を使った例文を示します。

[例1]　**Food prices have risen more than 75%.**
　　　食品価格は75％以上上昇した。

[例2]　**According to today's newspaper, the bank will raise interest rates.**
　　　本日の新聞によると、その銀行は金利を上げる予定である。

help leaking internal technologies という表現自体は誤りではないのですが、単語 leaking は leaking water（漏れている水）のように形容詞で使われることが多いため、読み手が、help（助ける）+ leaking internal technologies（漏れ出している内部の技術）と勘違いする可能性があります。
　以下のどちらかに修正することで適切な文になります。

[例3]　**～ allow technology to leak**
　　　技術の流出を可能にする

[例4] ～ inevitably result in technology leaking
必然的に、技術の流出をもたらす

06 backlash は、特定のイベント、意思決定や開発に対する強いリアクションに対して使われる単語です。benefit（恩恵、利益）に相対する語としては、disadvantage（不都合なこと）, burden（負担）, drawback（障害、難点）, detriment（不利益）などを使うのが適当です。

以下、backlash を使った例文を示します。

[例] The baseball player was a crowd favorite during the regular season but when he failed during the playoffs there was a strong supporter backlash.
その野球選手は公式戦のあいだは観客の人気者であったが、プレーオフで負けると、サポーターの強い反発が起きた。

添削反映バージョン

I think outsourcing overseas is generally a good idea.

As globalization progresses, business cannot be competitive without a global perspective.

Outsourcing is one of the important factors to lower the labor cost. Companies often replace their support staff or software developers with outsourced workers.

It may just raise the jobless rate in Japan, and allow technology to leak.

However, outsourcing creates new talents and opportunities in other countries. The balance between benefit and disadvantage should be always considered properly.

同テーマで講師が書き下ろしたバージョン

I think outsourcing overseas is generally a good idea.

Outsourcing is a key to reducing labor cost. In the present globalized age, companies routinely outsource manufacturing, IT and support staff function to lower-cost nations for considerable cost-benefit savings.

For the recipient nations, the benefits are more obvious still. Outsourcing is a valuable form of foreign direct investment that bolsters their middle class as well as leading them into the world economy.

The risks of outsourcing are real. Technology can easily leak and the job gains of one are the losses of another. But while the negatives of outsourcing must be always kept in mind, the social and economic stability of the world of nations that outsourcing brings is in every country's interest.

「同テーマで講師が書き下ろしたバージョン」語注

☐ **function**（動詞）「働く、機能する」

[例] I can't **function** until I have my first cup of coffee.

私は朝の一杯のコーヒーを飲むまで、働けない。

☐ **considerable**（形容詞）「相当な、多量の」

[例] I need to lose a **considerable** amount of weight.

私は体重をかなり減らす必要がある。

☐ **bolster**（動詞）「元気づける、鼓舞する」

[例] The government is trying many things to **bolster** the economy.

政府は景気を活気づけるために、たくさんのことを試みている。

各種英文ライティング試験 ①

TOEFL iBT®

[メンバー情報]
G.M. 様／大学生／25 歳

[文の説明]
　メリット、デメリット両方について述べ、現状では駅の建設は必要ないという結論に達しました。

　TOEFL（Test of English as a Foreign Language）は、アメリカの非営利教育団体 ETS（Educational Testing Service）によって運営されるテストで、アカデミックな英語運用能力テストとして最も信用度が高いと言われています。現在、世界 130 以上の国の 8000 以上の大学および団体で認可されています。英語を母語としない学習者の英語力を判定するものとして、最も高い信頼性を得ています。

　ETS は 2005 年 9 月より、さらに実践的な英語コミュニケーション能力の判定を目ざすものとして、TOEFL iBT（Internet-based Test）形式を導入しました。日本でも 2006 年 7 月からこの試験形式が実施されています。現在の TOEFL テストにおいては、従来行なっていた Paper-based Test (PBT), Computer-based Test (CBT) に代わって、この iBT 形式が中心になっています。

　そして TOEFL iBT の Writing セクションで、受験者の総合的英文処理能力およびライティングによるコミュニケーション能力が測定されます。Writing セクションには、Integrated Task（総合ライティング型問題）と、Independent Task（自由ライティング型問題）の 2 つが用意されています。Integrated Task はリスニングを含んでおり、ヘッドセットを使用して、解答します。そのため、この 20 分間の Integrated Task が先に行なわれ、そのあとヘッドセットをはずして、30 分間の Independent Task に入ります。

　ここでは、Independent Task の問題に挑戦しましょう。（英語便のサイトにも TOEFL iBT の Independent Task の練習問題を用意してありますので、ぜひそちらにも挑戦してみてください。）

　なお、TOEFL iBT では、問題文もすべて英語で提示されます。

問題

The local government has decided to build a new train station in your town. Discuss the pros and cons of this decision. Do you support or object to this plan?

原文

01. It seems that building a new train station has both advantages and disadvantages. While it may bring some benefit to the local people, we should take the downside into consideration as well.

02. The local government would claim that a new station will, above all, improve the convenience of the citizens. Having a new station in their neighborhood, a certain number of people will be able to use trains more easily. Since our town is located in a suburban area, many of the residents commute to school or work outside the town by train. Those who take a train every morning will be pleased if they have more stations in the town. Furthermore, more people might come to use trains for shopping and other affairs instead of using their own car, which will positively affect traffic and environmental problems. Another advantage of making a new station is that it could stimulate the local economy. Construction and management of a station will create new jobs, and shops and restaurants near the station will have more customers.

03. At the same time, however, there are some disadvantages that we should consider. First of all, it takes long time to make a new station and people living near the construction site will have to stand the noise and vibration until it has been completed. In addition, around the construction site there could arise a traffic jam owing to trucks and other vehicles and parents who have small children will be worried that their children might get in an accident.

04. Another problem regarding the new station is its cost. Making a new station will cost the government a great deal of money, most of which is from the tax revenue. The government should confirm that they will produce the benefit worth the cost.

05. What is important in deciding whether or not to build a new station is to weigh the advantages and disadvantages. Our town already has a train station, with which few people seem to be dissatisfied. Furthermore, we are faced with a financial problem because of the prolonged recession that our nation is suffering from. Considering the present situation, I would say that we don't need a new station for the time being. The government should make a decision at an appropriate time.

✍ 添削

01. It seems that building a new train station has both advantages and disadvantages. While it may bring some benefit to

the local people, we should take the downside into consideration as well.

---

02. The local government ~~would claim~~ claims that a new station will, above all, improve the convenience of the citizens. Having a new station in their neighborhood, ~~a certain number of~~ people will be able to use trains more easily. Since our town is located in ~~a suburban area~~ the suburbs, many of the residents commute to school or work outside the town by train. Those who take a train every morning will be pleased if ~~they have more stations~~ there is another station in the town. Furthermore, more people might ~~come to~~ use trains for shopping and other ~~affairs~~ things instead of ~~using~~ their own car, which will positively affect traffic and environmental problems associated with it. Another advantage of ~~making~~ building a new station is that it ~~could~~ will stimulate the local economy. Construction and management of a station will create new jobs, ~~and~~ giving shops and restaurants near the station ~~will have~~ more customers.

---

03. At the same time, however, there are some disadvantages that we should consider. First of all, it will ~~takes~~ take a long time to ~~make~~ build a new station and people living near the construction site will have to ~~stand~~ put up with the noise and vibration until ~~it~~ the station has been completed. In addition, around the construction site there ~~could arise~~ will be an increase in the number of ~~a~~ traffic ~~jam~~ jams ~~owing to trucks and other vehicles and~~. As a result, parents who have small children will be worried ~~that their children might get in an accident~~ about accidents.

---

04. Another problem regarding the new station is its cost. ~~Making~~ Building a new station will cost the government a great deal of money, most of which is from the tax revenue. The government should confirm that ~~they will produce the benefit worth the cost~~ the benefits will outweigh the cost.

---

05. What is important in deciding whether or not to build a new station is to weigh the advantages and disadvantages. Our town already has a train station~~, with which few people seem to be dissatisfied~~ that most people seem satisfied with. Furthermore, we are currently faced with a ~~financial problem because of the~~ prolonged recession that our nation is suffering from. Considering the present situation, I would say that we don't need a new station for the time being. The government should make a decision at an appropriate time.

👉 解説

02 地方自治体はすでに新しい駅の建設を決定しているため、would claim（主張しているだろう）ではなく、claims（主張する）とするのが適切です。

ここは、駅の利便性を主張している部分なので、people will be able to use trains more easily（人びとはもっと簡単に電車を使えるようになる）と、利点に焦点を置いて表現すべきです。a certain number of people（いくらかの人びと）とすると、意見を弱めてしまいます。

suburban area（郊外地域）より、suburbs（郊外地）がより広く使われています。

（1つの）新しい駅の建設が決定されているので、if they have more stations（彼らがもっと駅を持っていれば）ではなく、if there is another station（もう1つの駅があれば）とすべきです。

「もっとたくさんの人びとが電車を使うようになるかもしれません」という日本語から more people might come to use trains としたのだと思いますが、come to ～は、一定期間の推移や遷移を表わすときに使われる語句であるため、駅ができる前後の変化を表わすには不適切です。come to をはずして、more people might use trains（もっとたくさんの人が電車を使うかもしれません）のように表現するのが適切です。

以下、come to を使った例文を示します。

［例1］ **To come to a better understanding of classical music it's important to listen to the greats.**
クラシック音楽を理解できるようになるためには、偉大な音楽家（の音楽）を聴くことが重要である。

Eigobin Pointers　クラシック音楽を理解していくまでの期間を表わすため、come to が使われています。

単語 affair は「事柄、出来事」などもう少し特定のイベントを表わすときに使われるため、「買い物に行く」という日常のことに使うには不適切です。ここでは things が適当です。

以下、affair の利用例を示します。

［例2］ **I wanted the party to be a family affair.**
そのパーティは、家族のイベントであってほしかった。

文が more people might use ではじまっているので、instead of using（～を使う代わりに）と use を繰り返す必要はありません。instead of their own car（彼らの車の代わりに）と修正します。

environmental problems（環境問題）という言い方は意味が大きすぎるため、associated with it（それに関連した）と付け加えることで、「交通手段に関する環境問題」（CO_2 の削減など）と意味を特定できます。

making a station（駅を作る）より、building a station（駅を建設する）

という表現のほうがはっきりします。

　it could stimulate the local economy は、「それは地域の経済を活性化させるかもしれない」と日本語にすると、問題なく聞こえます。しかし、ここに could が使われていることで、ネイティブには「自信のない意見」に聞こえてしまいます。it will stimulate the local economy と will に書き換えれば、「それは地域の経済を活性化させるであろう」と明確に意見を述べる文になります。

　and が連続していて少し読みにくくなっています。後半を ~ giving shops and restaurants near the station more customers（駅の近くの店やレストランに多くの客をもたらす）に修正すれば、自然な文になります。

03　長くかかるのは将来のことなので、will を使います。また「長くかかる」は take a long time を使います。

　stand が「我慢する」という意味で使われる場合、通常、否定形（我慢できない）で用いられます。肯定文で「~に耐える、我慢する」という場合は、put up with ~ , または bear ~ をあてるのが適当です。

　以下、stand を使った例文を示します。

　　[例]　**I can't stand this noise coming from next door.**
　　　　　隣の部屋からの騒音が我慢できない。

　代名詞 it が construction site を指しているのか、new station を指しているのかあいまいです。the station と明記します。

　could ~（~かもしれない）と意見としてはあいまいな表現になっています。will に修正します。

　arise a traffic jam だと、渋滞が 1 つしか起きないようなニュアンスになります。an increase in the number of traffic jams（渋滞の数の増加）とすることで、随所に渋滞が発生する現象を表現できます。

traffic jam（渋滞）に、トラックや車が含まれることは周知の事実なので、owing to trucks and other vehicles の部分は冗長です。

　parents who ~ 以下の文は、「結果」なので、As a result（その結果と

して）を使って文を分割します。

　that their children might get in an accident（子供が事故に巻き込まれるかもしれないと）という部分は、文の前半から推測できるため、about accidents と短く簡潔に書くべきです。

04　「政府が裏付ける必要がある」のは、produce benefit（利益を生産する）ではなく、「利益がコストを上回ること」です。ここでは、the benefits will outweigh the cost（利益がコストを上回る）とするのが適当です。

05　with which few people seem to be dissatisfied（ほとんど不満に思っている人がいないようだ）は、that most people seem satisfied with（ほとんどの人が満足しているようだ）としたほうがわかりやすくなります。

　currently（現在は）を追加することで、現状の問題であることが明確になります。

　recession（景気後退）から、財政問題であることは明らかなので、financial problem because of the は冗長です。ここでは削除します。

添削反映バージョン

It seems that building a new train station has both advantages and disadvantages. While it may bring some benefit to the local people, we should take the downside into consideration as well.

The local government claims that a new station will, above all, improve the convenience of the citizens. Having a new station in their neighborhood, people will be able to use trains more easily. Since our town is located in the suburbs, many of the residents commute to school or work outside the town by train. Those who take a train every morning will be pleased if there is another station in the town. Furthermore, more people might use trains for shopping and other things instead of their own car, which will positively affect traffic and environmental problems associated with it. Another advantage of building a new station is that it will stimulate the local economy. Construction and management of a station will create new jobs, giving shops and restaurants near the station more customers.

At the same time, however, there are some disadvantages that we should consider. First of all, it will take a long time to build a new station and people living near the construction site will have to put up with the noise and vibration until the station has been completed. In addition, around the construction site there will be an increase in the number of traffic jams. As a result, parents who have small children will be worried about accidents.

Another problem regarding the new station is its cost. Building a new station will cost the government a great deal of money, most of which is from the tax revenue. The government should confirm that the benefits will outweigh the cost.

What is important in deciding whether or not to build a new station is to weigh the advantages and disadvantages. Our town already has a train station that most people seem satisfied with. Furthermore, we are currently faced with a prolonged recession that our nation is suffering from. Considering the present situation, I would say that we don't need a new station for the time being. The government should make a decision at an appropriate time.

> 同テーマで講師が書き下ろしたバージョン

Building a new train station has both advantages and disadvantages. While it may bring some benefits to the local community, we should take the downside into consideration as well.

The local government claims the new station will, above all, improve access to the train system. Since our town is located in the suburbs there are many commuters, and those who commute by train will be pleased if there is another station. Furthermore, additional people will use the train network for shopping and other daily activities, instead of using their car, positively impacting traffic density and associated environmental concerns.

Another advantage of making the new station is the stimulation of the local economy. Construction and management of the station will create new jobs, while the shops and restaurants that are located near the station will benefit from an influx of foot traffic.

There are, however, some disadvantages that we should consider. First of all, it takes a long time to build a new station because construction needs to be worked around the operation of the existing schedule of trains. People living near the site will therefore have to put up with noise and vibration for a considerable period of time. Traffic congestion around the site will also increase due to the presence of trucks and other vehicles related to the construction.

A further problem is cost. The local government will have to contribute towards the construction costs and this could add up to a great deal of money. It is not clear if the local government can be sure that this expenditure of tax revenue will produce benefits that justify the cost.

It is important to weigh the advantages and disadvantages when deciding whether or not to build the new train station. While our town has only a single station at present, most people seem satisfied with it. Furthermore, we are presently enduring financial problems related to the prolonged recession. Considering the present realities, I would say that the proposal to build a new station does not seem feasible, but that the government should reevaluate the proposal after economic conditions have improved.

「同テーマで講師が書き下ろしたバージョン」語注

☐ **influx**（名詞）「流入、流れ込むこと」
　[例]　**Canada has had an influx of immigrants in recent years.**
　　　カナダは近年多くの移住者をかかえている。

☐ **foot traffic**「客の出足」
　foot traffic には、「歩行者、徒歩での交通」という意味もありますが、講師は「客の出足」という意味で使っています。
　[例]　**The sushi shop near my house is very busy because it gets a lot of foot traffic.**
　　　私の家の近くのすし屋は、客の出足がよく、とても忙しい。

☐ **congestion**（名詞）「密集、充満、混雑、過密」
　［例］　**The Internet seems slow today, there must be a lot of congestion.**
　　　今日はインターネットが遅いようだ。かなり混雑しているに違いない。

☐ **add up**「計算が合う、帳尻が合う」
　［例］　**Jenny was busy dealing with a lot of customers, and at the end of the day the receipts didn't add up.**
　　　ジェニーはたくさんのお客の対応で忙しかったため、1日の終わりには収入が合わなくなっていた。

各種英文ライティング試験 ②

英検1級

[メンバー情報]
吉田　茂子様／その他／59歳

[文の説明]
インターネットにおいての学習効果を中心に意見をまとめてみました。

英検（実用英語技能検定）1級では、1次試験の筆記で英作文問題が1問出題されます。100分の筆記試験の最後の問題になりますので、受験者はこの英作文問題に十分に時間をかけられるように、時間配分を考えて問題を解き進める必要があります。

英検の英作文では、指定されたトピックについて、200語程度で書きます。そして6つのポイントが与えられますので、そのうちの3つを使って作文します。序論（introduction）と結論（conclusion）を含む3つのパラグラフ以上の文書にすることが求められます。

出題されるテーマは、現代の社会問題を扱ったものがほとんどです。テクノロジーや環境問題、国際事情、あるいは現代人のモラルといったことなど、現代の社会問題について、幅広く出題されます。過去に出題された問題を集めた対策本も出ていますので、受験前に確認しておく必要があるでしょう。

それでは、ここで、英検1級の英作文問題にチャレンジしてみましょう。（英語便のサイトには、ほかにも英検1級の練習問題を用意してありますので、ぜひそちらにもチャレンジしてみてください。）

英検の問題の指示文も、TOEFL iBT や TOEIC SW テスト同様、英語で書かれています。

問題

TOPIC: Has the Internet improved the way we study?

原文

01. It's obvious that the Internet has improved the way we study. As someone who studies on the Internet, I'd like to describe the fact from these three points: time, money, opportunity.

02. Firstly, the Internet has allowed us to have great access to information. We can get almost every information on the Internet without wasting time, almost all through the world. It was impossible many years ago.

03. Secondly, we can save money by using the Internet. We can share many images, lots of knowledge, culture, without buying them. We can listen to a lecture taken place in a college while at home. We can send our writings or tests and get the results online immediately after taking correspondence courses. Neither fare nor postage occurs. Thus it is easier to study than before.

04. Thirdly, as there are so many learning sites on the Internet for free or at reasonable prices. We have more opportunities to learn than ever. Also, people on the same learning site can interact by talking on the bulletin board, competing together for achieving points or scores, exchanging emails. Interaction is a positive factor that helps users learn.

05. In conclusion, the Internet is a must for people who want to study more effectively. It is expected to accumulate quality information to build information dependability and become

more innovative on and on.

✎ 添削

01. It's obvious that the Internet has improved the way we study. As someone who studies ~~on~~ using the Internet, I'd like to describe ~~the fact~~ why I believe this is true from these three points of view: time, money, opportunity.

---

02. Firstly, the Internet has allowed us ~~to have great~~ easy access to a lot of information. We can get almost ~~every~~ any information on the Internet without wasting time, almost ~~all through~~ everywhere in the world. It was impossible many years ago.

---

03. Secondly, we can save money by using the Internet. We can share many images, ~~lots of~~ a lot of knowledge, and culture, without ~~buying them~~ paying any money. We can listen to a lecture ~~taken~~ taking place in a college while at home. We can send our writings or tests and get the results online immediately after taking correspondence courses. ~~Neither fare nor postage occurs~~ We do not have to pay any fares or postage costs. Thus it is easier to study than before.

---

04. Thirdly, as there are so many learning sites on the Internet which can be used for free or ~~at~~ for reasonable prices. We have more opportunities to learn than ever. Also, people on the same learning site can interact by talking on a bulletin board, competing ~~together for achieving points or scores~~ for points, or exchanging emails. Interaction is a positive factor

that helps users learn.

---

05. In conclusion, the Internet is a must for people who want to study more effectively. It is expected ~~to~~ that the Internet will accumulate quality information to build information dependability and become more innovative ~~on and on~~.

👉 解説

01 on the Internet（インターネットで）はよく使われる表現ですが、「インターネットを使って〜」とインターネットを道具として考えるような場合は、using the Internet というような表現を使えばいいでしょう。

以下、例文を示します。

[例1]　**Here are three ways to save time using the Internet.**
　　　インターネットを使って時間を節約する3つの方法を挙げます。

エッセイのイントロダクションでは、後続で伝えていく内容の主旨を提示します。事実を引用することはあっても、本論で実際に記述される内容は「私は〜だと思う」という自分の考えです。このため、I'd like to describe the fact（事実を説明する）という表現は不適切です。

ここでは、以下のような表現を使うのが適当です。

[例2]　**I'd like to describe why I believe this is true.**
　　　どうしてそれがほんとうであると信じるのか説明します。

[例3]　**I'd like to describe why I believe this to be the case.**
　　　なぜ、その通りだと思うのか、説明します。

「〜の観点から」と言う場合は、from 〜 points of view という表現を使い

ます。また、「〜の視点より」「〜を要点として」という、以下のような表現も可能です。

[例4]　**〜 from these three perspectives: time, money, opportunity**
時間・お金・機会の３つの視点より〜

[例5]　**〜 using these three points as headings to support my opinion.**
３つのポイントを私の意見をサポートする要点として〜

02　great access は「すごいアクセス」というように読み手にとって、いろいろな意味に解釈できるあいまいな表現です。ここではもう少し具体的な、easy（容易な）, a lot of（多くの）などの単語を利用すれば、もっとわかりやすくなります。

information（情報）は不可算名詞です。every は可算名詞にのみ使うことができる形容詞であるため、ここでは any information（どんな情報でも）という表現が適切です。

all through the world は不自然な英語表現です。「世界中で」という意味を表わすときは、一般的に以下のようなものを使います。

throughout the world
all over the world
globally
worldwide
everywhere in the world

03　lots of は口語表現であり、a lot of に比べてカジュアルに聞こえます。アカデミックエッセイでは a lot of が適しています。

３つの語句を列挙する際は、スタイルの観点から、最後の語句の前には and を挿入します。以下、例文を示します。

[例1]　**Apples, oranges and grapes provide carbohydrates, vitamins and minerals.**
　　　りんご、みかん、ぶどうは炭水化物、ビタミン、ミネラルを提供します。

We can share many images, lots of knowledge, and culture, without buying them. という文は、最後の them が images, knowledge, culture を指していますが、buying culture（文化を買う）という表現は不自然です。ここでは、without buying them を without paying any money（お金をまったくかけずに）と修正するのがいいと思います。

take place（行なわれる、開催される）は能動態で用いられるため、受動態の taken ではなく、現在分詞の taking を使う必要があります。take place の利用例を説明します。

[例2]　**The lecture took place yesterday.**
　　　その講演は昨日開催された。

occur は「発生する」という意味の単語ですが、「料金が発生する」という日本語の英訳には使えません。ここでは、「料金が発生しない」を We do not have to pay ～（～を支払う必要がない）とすれば、適切な文になります。

04　for free（無料の）は、副詞であるため、動詞は修飾できますが、various learning sites for free のような形で名詞を修飾することはできません。ここでは、which can be used というセンテンスを挿入して、for free が使えるように文を変換する必要があります。
　以下、for free の用例を示します。

[例1]　**I found books I could download for free.**
　　　無料でダウンロードできる本を見つけた。
　Eigobin Pointers　「ダウンロードする」という動詞を修飾しています。

competing together for achieving points or scores の部分は英語表現

として意味が取りにくく、不自然です。
　scoreは、テストの点数やスポーツの試合の点数など、何かの過程や努力をした結果得られたものに対して使われます。

［例2］　**In the test we are given a final score.**

　一方pointは、クレジットカードのポイントのように、ある時点で得られてもまた増えつづけるようなものに使われます。

［例3］　**When we go to an electronics retail store, we are given points.**

　ここでは、compete for points（ポイントを競い合う）, またはscore point（ポイントを手に入れる）といった表現にすれば、わかりやすくなります。

05 「〜であることが期待される」と表現したいときは、It is expected that S V という構文で対応するのがいいと思います。
　on and on （長々と、どこまでも）という表現は、終わりのない延々とつづくような事象に対して使われます。一方、become 〜（〜になる）には、一定のものに到達する意味があります。このため、on and onとbecomeが1つの文で使われることはありません。また、on and onは通常、動詞の直後に置かれます。
　以下、on and onの利用例を示します。

［例］　**She goes on and on after she has a few drinks.**
　　　少し飲むと、彼女は永遠に話しつづける。

添削反映バージョン

It's obvious that the Internet has improved the way we study. As someone who studies using the Internet, I'd like to describe why I believe this is true from these three points of view: time, money, opportunity.

Firstly, the Internet has allowed us easy access to a lot of information. We can get almost any information on the Internet without wasting time, almost everywhere in the world. It was impossible many years ago.

Secondly, we can save money by using the Internet. We can share many images, a lot of knowledge, and culture, without paying any money. We can listen to a lecture taking place in a college while at home. We can send our writings or tests and get the results online immediately after taking correspondence courses. We do not have to pay any fares or postage costs. Thus it is easier to study than before.

Thirdly, as there are so many learning sites on the Internet which can be used for free or for reasonable prices. We have more opportunities to learn than ever. Also, people on the same learning site can interact by talking on a bulletin board, competing for points, or exchanging emails. Interaction is a positive factor that helps users learn.

In conclusion, the Internet is a must for people who want to study more effectively. It is expected that the Internet will accumulate quality information to build information dependability and become more innovative.

> 同テーマで講師が書き下ろしたバージョン

The Internet has, without doubt, changed the way we get information. As someone who studies on the Internet, I'd like to support this statement under the three banners of 'time', 'money', and 'opportunity'.

Firstly, the Internet gives access to a wealth of information. We can find pretty much anything through the Internet, instantaneously: the news, instructional sites, social networks, auction sites, videos, the list goes on and on.

Secondly, we can save money by using the Internet: we can share images, knowledge, cultural interests, guides, and share music, all without putting our hands in our pockets. We can listen to lectures from the comfort of our own homes. We can get our results online immediately when taking correspondence courses. In short, we can forego the time and cost of using public transportation and postal services.

Finally, as there are so many educational sites for next to nothing, we have more opportunities to learn than ever. These sites also have bulletin boards offering points to members who are actively involved in the site through comments and emails. Interaction is the key to overall improvement. There is no excuse for having no time to study.

In conclusion, the Internet is a must for people who want to study more and more. It will undoubtedly go on accumulating reliable information and continue to become more innovative.

「同テーマで講師が書き下ろしたバージョン」語注

☐ **without doubt**「間違いなく、まぎれもなく」
[例] **Without doubt, he is going to be the next CEO.**
間違いなく、彼は次のCEOになるだろう。

☐ **banner**（名詞）「大儀、理念」
banner は元々「国旗、軍旗」という意味ですが、「大儀、理念」という意味でよく使われます。
[例] **The candidate is running on a banner of fiscal responsibility.**
その候補者は財政責任を理念として立候補している。

☐ **instantaneously**（副詞）「即座に、瞬間的に」
[例] **Nowadays news stories seem to reach the Internet instantaneously.**
今日では、ニュースは瞬時にインターネットに届くように見える。

☐ **without putting our hands in our pockets**「お金を使わずに」
「お金を使わずに」という意味では without using any money という表現も使えます。

☐ **next to nothing**「ほとんどなきに等しい、ただも同然で、限りなくただ

に近く」

　next to nothing は文字通り、nothing の隣ということで、nearly nothing（ゼロではないが、ゼロに近い）という意味になります。

[例]　**I did next to nothing my whole summer vacation.**
　　　夏休みをとおしてほとんど何もしなかった。

各種英文ライティング試験 ③

TOEIC SW® テスト

[メンバー情報]
Y.N. 様／その他／55 歳

[文の説明]
財政難のなか、コミュニティセンター修復に賛成する意見をまとめました。

　TOEIC SW テスト（TOEIC Speaking and Writing Test）は、2007 年 1 月に第 1 回公開テストが実施されました。従来のリスニング・リーディングの問題からなる TOEIC テストとは別に、スピーキングとライティングの能力を測定・評価するテストとして、今後ますます受験者の拡大が予想されます。

　試験は、ETS 認定テスト会場のパソコンで受験します。ヘッドセットを装着し、画面の指示に従い、スピーキングでは音声を吹き込み、ライティングでは文章をタイプして解答します。そして表現として理解できる範囲であれば、多少の言い間違いやスペルミスは減点されません。詳しくは公式ホームページ（http://www.toeic.or.jp/sw/）でご確認ください。

　このテストは、スピーキング・テスト、ライティング・テストとも、200 点満点です。ライティングでは、「写真描写問題」（Write a sentence based on a picture）[5 問出題され、8 分で答える。指定された 2 つの語句を使い、写真にあう文を作成する]、「E メール作成問題」（Respond to a written request）[2 問、各 10 分。E メールを読み、返信のメールを作成する]、「意見を記述する問題」（Write an opinion essay）[1 問、30 分。テーマについての意見と理由を記述する] の 3 題が出題されます。

　英語便のサイトでは、「E メール作成問題」と「意見を記述する問題」を用意していますが、ここでは「意見を記述する問題」に挑戦してみましょう。

　この問題では、提示されたテーマについて、論拠や例を示しながら自分の考えを文書にします。語数に制限はありませんが、高い評価を得るには 300 語以上が目安となります。そして具体的には、以下の点が問われます。●適切な説明、例、詳細が示され、よく構成されているか。●論理の発展性、一貫性があるか。●多様な構文、適切な語彙、語句、慣用句を使っているか。

　では、さっそく問題に挑戦しましょう。本番では、問題文も含めてすべて英語で提示されます。

問題

Your neighborhood is going to cancel the annual summer festival in order to save money. The money saved will be spent on renovating the community center. Do you think the money should be used for renovating the community center? Give clear reasons and/or examples to support your opinion.

原文

01. First off, I must admit it's a great shame to forgo the summer festival. It plays a significant role to keep our community closely knitted, to say nothing of the fun it offers to kids.

02. However, we can't turn a blind eye to the aging community center any longer. It's a long-standing agenda but we tend to put it on the back-burner since we are always deluged with urgent businesses to address immediately.

03. On top of that, we know too well the renovation business costs us an arm and a leg, which is quite daunting, because, as is often the case, we are hard-pressed budget-wise. At the same time, there's no denying that we can't just let the building go run-down by twiddling our thumbs.

04. The community center is too vital for us to lose. Without it, our community won't be able to function properly. In order

to maintain a nice neighborhood, we need to stay in touch on a regular basis. It's essential for us to get together at the community center to talk things over, reach consensus and take collective actions.

05. For example, we have to protect our neighborhood from local crimes, such as household burglaries and child molesting cases. We may need to organize vigilante groups to patrol the area. We meet up at the community center when a crisis hits and sort things out. It serves as a nerve center to deal with various issues in the community.

06. It also provides space to store communal stuff, such as sashes or uniforms for local volunteers, collapsible chairs and tents for summer festivals and so on. It can be our designated evacuation center in case of earthquakes and other natural disasters, keeping bottled water, emergency food, first-aid kits and the like.

07. It all comes down to prioritizing matters as far as budget allocation goes. This time around, I'm afraid we have to set the money aside for the renovation. As for the summer festival, let's devise some other plans. We may come up with an ingenious, brilliant idea which would cost nothing, but turn out to be a good fun.

✎ 添削

01. First off, I must admit it's a great shame to forgo the summer festival. It plays a significant role ~~to keep~~ in keeping our community ~~closely knitted~~ close-knit, to say nothing of the fun it offers to kids.

---

02. However, we can't turn a blind eye to the aging community center any longer. It's a long-standing ~~agenda~~ problem but we tend to put it on the back-burner since we are always deluged with urgent ~~businesses~~ business to address immediately.

---

03. On top of that, we know too well the renovation ~~business costs~~ will cost us an arm and a leg, which is quite daunting, because, as is often the case, we are hard-pressed budget-wise. At the same time, there's no denying that we can't just let the building ~~go~~ become run-down by twiddling our thumbs.

---

04. The community center is too vital for us to lose. Without it, our community won't be able to function properly. In order to maintain a nice neighborhood, we need to stay in touch on a regular basis. It's essential for us to get together at the community center to talk things over, reach consensus and take collective ~~actions~~ action.

---

05. For example, we have to protect our neighborhood from local crimes, such as household burglaries and child ~~molesting~~ molestation ~~cases~~. We may need to organize ~~vigilante~~ local patrol groups to patrol the area. We meet up at the

community center when a crisis hits and sort things out. It serves as a nerve center to deal with various issues in the community.

---

06. It also provides space to store communal ~~stuff~~ equipment, such as sashes or uniforms for local volunteers, collapsible chairs and tents for summer festivals and so on. It ~~can be~~ is our designated evacuation center in case of earthquakes and other natural disasters, keeping bottled water, emergency food, first-aid kits and the like.

---

07. It all comes down to prioritizing matters as far as budget allocation goes. This time around, I'm afraid we have to set the money aside for the renovation. As for the summer festival, let's devise some other plans. We may come up with an ingenious, brilliant idea which would cost nothing, but turn out to be ~~a~~ good fun.

👉 解説

01　「〜で役割を果たす」は、play a role in 〜ing というように、前置詞 in を使います。keep は keeping とします。

　closely knitted（緊密に結びついている）という英語表現は誤りではありませんが、形容詞の close-knit（結びつきの強い）のほうがより一般的です。

02　agenda は「検討すべき課題の一覧」という意味で、通常は複数の項目を含みます。ここでは1つの項目 the aging community center を指しているため、problem（問題）または agenda list（アジェンダの項目）とするべきです。

「ビジネス、商売、商取引」の意味で business という単語を使うときは、通常単数形にします。

Eigobin Pointers business を「会社、事務所」という意味で使うときは、複数形を使うことができます。

[例] **He has a lot of businesses.**
彼はたくさんの会社を持っています。

03 ここでは、renovation（修復）のみで意味が通じます。
renovation business のような XXXXX business という表記は、口語表現では、XXXXX thing のような感覚で、すべて含んでいることを言及する形で使われることがあります。以下、例を挙げて説明します。

[例1] **My restaurant business is struggling in this down economic climate.**
私のレストランビジネス（レストラン経営、レストランへの物品販売、またはレストランの清掃など関連するものすべて）は、不況のなか、奮闘している。

このように、business を付けてしまうと、読み手にカジュアルに響いたり、意図するものより広義な意味を連想させてしまうこともあるため、注意して用いなければなりません。

renovation「修復」は未来に行なわれるため、will を挿入します。
「（一定の期間を経て）荒廃する、疲れきる」は、go run-down ではなく、become run-down と通常 become を使用します。
動詞 become を使うことで、「〜になる」という一定期間をかけて変化することが伝わります。以下、例文を示します。

[例2] **The hotel became run-down and was eventually demolished.**
そのホテルは荒廃し、最終的に取り壊された。

04 action は不可算名詞です。「一般の行動・アクションという概念」を表わすときには、actions と複数にせず、単数形 action を使います。

Eigobin Pointers しかし、以下のように、「複数の行動・アクション(パターン)」がある場合は actions を使うことができます。

[例] **Military actions are often the testing ground for new technology.**
軍事行動は、新技術の実験材料となることが多い。

05 「幼児虐待、子供に対するいたずら」は、child molestation と表現します。

vigilante group は日本語では「自警団」ですが、英語では「地元の法律や警察に不満を持つ人びとが自主的に組織化するようなグループ」を指すため、日本の地元ボランティアグループとはイメージが異なります。ここでは、local patrol group という表現が適しています。

06 単語 stuff（物）は文の全体のトーンに対してカジュアルすぎます。ここでは equipment（設備）が適切です。

It can be our designated evacuation center は、日本語にすると、「私たちの指定の避難所になりえるかもしれない」と何の問題もなく見えますが、備品を揃えることで避難所になることがすでに決まっているのであれば、it is our designated evacuation center（私たちの指定の避難所になります）とすべきです。

07 名詞の fun（楽しみ）は不可算名詞であり、冠詞は不要です。

添削反映バージョン

First off, I must admit it's a great shame to forgo the summer festival. It plays a significant role in keeping our community close-knit, to say nothing of the fun it offers to kids.

However, we can't turn a blind eye to the aging community center any longer. It's a long-standing problem but we tend to put it on the back-burner since we are always deluged with urgent business to address immediately.

On top of that, we know too well the renovation will cost us an arm and a leg, which is quite daunting, because, as is often the case, we are hard-pressed budget-wise. At the same time, there's no denying that we can't just let the building become run-down by twiddling our thumbs.

The community center is too vital for us to lose. Without it, our community won't be able to function properly. In order to maintain a nice neighborhood, we need to stay in touch on a regular basis. It's essential for us to get together at the community center to talk things over, reach consensus and take collective action.

For example, we have to protect our neighborhood from local crimes, such as household burglaries and child molestation. We may need to organize local patrol groups to patrol the area. We meet up at the community center when a crisis hits and sort things out. It serves as a nerve center to deal with various issues in the community.

It also provides space to store communal equipment, such as sashes or uniforms for local volunteers, collapsible chairs and tents for summer festivals and so on. It is our designated evacuation center in case of earthquakes and other natural disasters, keeping bottled water, emergency food, first-aid kits and the like.

It all comes down to prioritizing matters as far as budget allocation goes. This time around, I'm afraid we have to set the money aside for the renovation. As for the summer festival, let's devise some other plans. We may come up with an ingenious, brilliant idea which would cost nothing, but turn out to be good fun.

同テーマで講師が書き下ろしたバージョン

First off, I must admit it's a great shame to forgo the summer festival. It plays a significant role in keeping our community close-knit, to say nothing of the fun it offers to kids.

However, we can't turn a blind eye to the aging community center any longer. It's a long-standing problem which we are forever putting on the back burner since we are always deluged with other business in need of urgent attention.

On top of that, we know too well the renovation will costs us an arm and a leg, which is quite daunting, because, as is often the case, we are hard-pressed budget-wise. At the same time, there's no denying that we can't continue to just twiddle our thumbs and allow the building to deteriorate.

The community center is too vital for us to lose. Without it, our community won't be able to function properly. In order to keep our neighborhood harmonious, safe and livable, we need to stay in touch on a regular basis. It's essential for us to get together at the community center to talk things over, reach consensus and take collective action.

For example, we have to protect our neighborhood from crimes such as household burglary and child molestation. In the future, we might need to organize neighborhood patrols. We meet up at the community center when these kinds of issues arise. It serves as a nerve center from which to deal with various issues in the community.

The community center also provides space to store equipment, such as collapsible chairs and tents for summer festivals, and so on. It is our designated evacuation center in case of earthquakes and other natural disasters; our storehouse of bottled water, emergency food, first-aid kits and the like.

In the end, it all comes down to prioritizing. This time around, I'm afraid, we have to set the money aside for the renovation. As for the summer festival, let's devise some other plans. We may come up with an ingenious idea which would cost us nothing, but be great fun.

「同テーマで講師が書き下ろしたバージョン」語注

□ **back burner**（名詞）「(計画などの) 棚上げ」

back burner は、キッチンのコンロからきている用語で、2列あるうちのうしろのバーナーは前にあるメインバーナーに比べ、弱い火力でぐつぐつ煮たりするときなどにおもに使われることから、「棚上げ」の意味に使われています。

[例] **Until the market stabilizes, we should put the project on the back burner.**

市場が安定化するまで、そのプロジェクトは棚上げにすべきだ。

□ **hard-pressed**（形容詞）「追い詰められている、四苦八苦している」

[例] **You would be hard-pressed to find a restaurant at this time of night.**

夜のこの時間では、レストランを探すのに苦労しますよ。

□ **-wise**「〜のように、〜の方向に、〜の点で、〜に関しては、〜的に、〜風に」

[例1] **Cost-wise, upgrading our computers is not an option.**

コスト面から、コンピュータのアップグレードという選択肢はない。

[例2] **The film wasn't very good story-wise.**

その映画はストーリーに関してはあまりよくなかった。

□ **twiddle one's thumbs**「(暇なので) のんびりしている」

両手を組んで、親指をくるくる回しているしぐさから、退屈で何もしていない状況を表わすときに使われています。

[例] **The boss was out of the office for a meeting so I twiddled my thumbs for a while.**

上司がミーティングで外出中だったので、しばらくのんびりしていた。

□ **vital**（形容詞）「きわめて重要な、なくてはならない」

[例] **When it comes to dealing with climate change, international cooperation is vital.**

気候変動への取り組みに関しては、国際協力が不可欠である。

□ **nerve center**「組織などの中枢（部）」
　[例]　**Research and development should be the nerve center of the industry.**
　　　研究開発は、企業の中枢であるべきだ。

□ **and the like**「〜など」
and the like は etc. と同様の意味ですが、やや形式ばった表現になります。

□ **ingenious**（形容詞）「独創性のある、工夫に富んでいる、思いつきのよい」
ingenious は普通は思いつかないようなすごいアイデアや物事によく使われます。
　[例]　**Solar panels are an ingenious way to store energy.**
　　　ソーラーパネルは、エネルギーを蓄える独創的な方法である。

III.
英語便添削
チャレンジ編
CHALLENGING COURSE

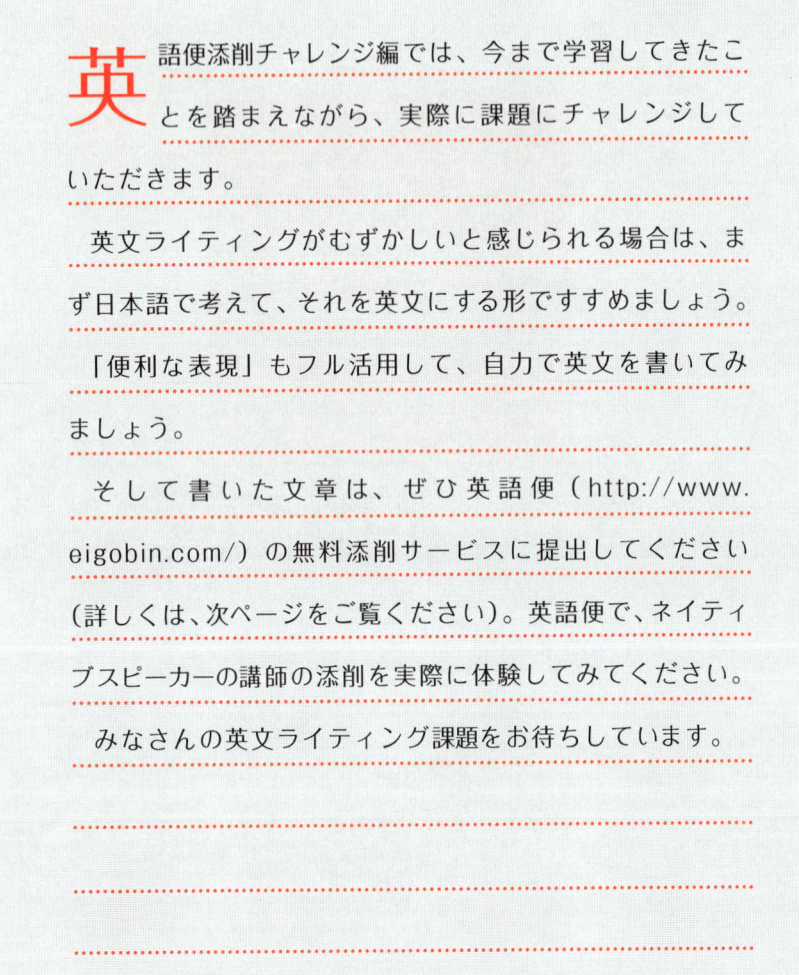

英語便添削チャレンジ編では、今まで学習してきたことを踏まえながら、実際に課題にチャレンジしていただきます。

　英文ライティングがむずかしいと感じられる場合は、まず日本語で考えて、それを英文にする形ですすめましょう。

　「便利な表現」もフル活用して、自力で英文を書いてみましょう。

　そして書いた文章は、ぜひ英語便（http://www.eigobin.com/）の無料添削サービスに提出してください（詳しくは、次ページをご覧ください）。英語便で、ネイティブスピーカーの講師の添削を実際に体験してみてください。

　みなさんの英文ライティング課題をお待ちしています。

課題

ここでは、課題を読んで実際に英文を書いてみます。

添削で学習してきたことを踏まえて、実際に課題に挑戦してみてください。短い英文でも、時制や冠詞などのニュアンス、また、文の全体のトーンや読み手に与える印象に気を配りながら、できるだけ自然な英語を書くように心がけてください。

英語便の無料添削

課題は3つ用意しました。3つの課題のうち、1つを英語便の無料添削サービスにご提出いただけます。

課題を提出する際、インターネットメールアドレスが必要です。

課題の提出は、インターネット上の画面から行ないます。英語便より、ご登録いただいたメールアドレスに、添削結果の確認方法をご案内いたします。

そしてそのページでキーワードの入力が求められますので、以下の文字と数字を入力してください。

kenkyushaeigobin201201

実際の英語便の添削は、ネイティブスピーカーの講師が英語で直接解説しています。英語のコメントを読むのは、はじめはむずかしく感じられるかもしれませんが、慣れてくると意外と英語の説明のほうがニュアンスがわかりやすく、楽しく学習していただけると思います。

英文の準備ができたら、英語便のホームページ www.eigobin.com にアクセスしてください。本書購入者用の課題提出ページをご用意しています。

[課題1]　ビジネスメール
[課題2]　プライベートメール
[課題3]　ショートエッセイ

[課題1]

✉ ビジネスメール

あなたは、小売店を経営しています。現在、新しい商品の取り扱いを検討しています。

商品の取り扱い先へメールを出して、仕入れに関する内容を問い合わせてください。

問い合わせの内容は、商品の詳細、価格、発送方式など何でもかまいません。

（参考⇨「ネイティブ添削実践編」ビジネスメール②──商品の問い合わせ）

👉 便利な表現

Could you tell me dimensions?（寸法を教えていただけますか？）
Would it be possible to get a better discount?
（値引きしていただくことは可能ですか？）
I would like to know when it will arrive.
（それがいつ到着するのか知りたいです。）
We are wondering how long it will take.
（どれくらい期間がかかるのか知りたいと思っています。）
Do you know which courier was used?
（どの宅配業者に仕事が発注されたのか、ご存知ですか？）

課題サンプル

Dear Mr. Baker,

I run a small retail store that specializes in kitchen gadgets. I'm expanding into dishes and would like to carry your line. I would like to inquire about shipping. Could you tell me the average shipping time to our location? Would it be possible to receive an order within 24 hours? I'm also wondering about breakage. I would like to know if it is possible to credit my account instead of shipping a replacement. I look forward to hearing from you.

Sincerely,

David Leach

Gourmet Gizmos

[語注]
※ carry　店に置く・在庫として持つ
※ breakage　破損

［課題2］
🏠 プライベートメール

友人の Dave を、2泊3日の国内旅行へ誘ってください。日付と行き先を自由に設定して、Dave が旅行に行きたくなるように誘い出してください。

（参考⇨「ネイティブ添削実践編」プライベートメール③──旅行に誘う）

👉 便利な表現

Why don't you go to the restaurant?（そのレストランに行かない？）
How about going to karaoke?（カラオケ行かない？）
Would you care to join us?（一緒に行かない？）
Just bring yourself.（手ぶらで来てください。）
Please feel free to drop in anytime.
　（いつでも気軽に遊びに来てください。）
The more the merrier.（人数が多いほうが楽しいよ。）
It should be a good time.（楽しいと思うよ。）
It'll be on me.（おごるよ。）
Would you like to come with me?（一緒に行きたい？）

課題サンプル

Hi Dave,

How's it going? I'm getting a little burned-out from work. Actually, I'm thinking of going on an onsen trip during Golden Week. Are you interested? I figure I'll go for two nights (maybe the 4th and 5th). I know a great place in Tochigi near Nikko. It's about two and a half hours from here. It has got great outdoor baths. There is a beautiful view overlooking the river and it's not all that expensive. I thought you might be up for it. I'm going to book it tomorrow, so let me know if you are in or not before then.
I hope you can make it.

Koji

[語注]
※ burned-out　疲れきった
※ not all that　それほど〜ない
※ up for 〜　　〜したい

[課題3]

🏛 ショートエッセイ

The popularity of ebooks has grown dramatically over the last couple of years. However, not everyone is happy about this. Traditionalists believe that nothing can replace the convenience of paper books and that ebooks are somehow less 'real' than paper books. On the other hand, many techies believe ebooks are the future of reading and far more versatile than books. What do you think about the future of books? Do you think ebooks are the future of reading or just a passing fad?

(参考⇨「ネイティブ添削実践編」ショートエッセイ——問題点をまとめる)

👉 便利な表現

I believe it's the right thing to do.
(私はそれが正しいことだと信じています。)
That being said, 〜(それはそうだが・そうは言っても)
On the other hand, 〜 (一方〜)
I would say it's a good idea to use public transportation.
(公共交通手段を使うことは、いいアイデアだと思います。)
Imagine a world without books.
(本のない世界をイメージしてみてください。)
A good example would be having a mobile phone.
(1つの例は、携帯を持つことです。)

> 課題サンプル

Personally, I don't think the ebooks will be a straight replacement for paper books. There will always be some people who want to feel the paper in their hands and physically turn the pages instead of tapping or swiping a screen. That being said, I see ebooks as a great way to enhance the reading experience. Ebooks can easily contain all kinds of content. Imagine being able to click on a word to start some background music as you read about the main character walking into a nightclub. Or maybe you could click on another word and see an image of what the character is looking at. Click on a video to see what's in the character's mind. These possibilities lead me to believe that ebooks are definitely here to stay. They won't replace paper books, but will give us a totally new way to read. I can't wait.

重要英語表現索引 INDEX

※本文中の赤字にした部分を中心に拾いました。

A

absolutely 14
absorb 90
action 199, 202
actions → we are displeased with the actions of ～
add up 183-84
advance → in advance
affair 178
after authentication 113
after being authorized 113
agenda list 200
a little 14
all ～ 119
all of the ～ 119
all over the world 189
all set → I'm all set.
a lot of 189
also 5
and 3, 189-90
and the like 205, 207
angry 14
another 53
any information 189
anytime 163; → Please feel free to drop in anytime.
appreciate (I would appreciate it if ～) 61
appreciated → it would be greatly appreciated
arrive → I would like to know when it will arrive.
as a gratitude of ～ 39

as a result 176, 179
as a token of ～ 37-38
Attention (Attn:/ ATTN:) 77
at the moment 147, 149
at this time 67, 69
at your office 33, 35
authentication → after authentication
authorized → after being authorized
awful 14

B

back burner 204, 206
backlash 170
banner 193-94
bear ～ 179
become ～ 191, 199, 201
become run-down 201
beg 133
beg for 133
be giving 133
be off to ～ 144-45
be rushed off my feet 144-45
best regards 20
bolster 171-72
both (both A and B) 10
both options 59, 62
breakage 213
burden 170
burned-out 215
business 199, 201
businesses 201
buy you 134
by car 141

218

C

camping → go camping
can't find any words to express   127
car → by car
carry   213
change   114
charge for ~   62
child molestation   202
claims   176-77
close-knit   199-200
come and visit   141
come by   35
come to   178
come with → Would you like to come with me?
command → give command to
compete for points   191
complain → I'm writing to you to complain about ~
complaint → we have a complaint with ~
completely   14
conclude   72-73
conference call   22-23
congestion   182, 184
considerable   171-72
continued   67-68
cooperation → Thank you for your cooperation.
could   26, 29
could you let me know   62
Could you tell me dimensions?   212
courier → Do you know which courier was used?
courtesy   81
cover (all)   51-52, 149
currently   177, 180

D

dear   33-34
describe   188
desired → if desired
detail → for details

detriment   170
dimensions → Could you tell me dimensions?
disadvantage   170
discount → Would it be possible to get a better discount?
displeased → we are displeased with the actions of ~
do (all)   149
do homework   140
don't hesitate to ~   70
doubt → without doubt
Do you know which courier was used?   212
drawback   170
drop by   34-35

E

easy   187, 189
efficient   93
effort (their efforts have recently been rewarded)   86
email or call me   163
enhance   114
equipment   200, 202
especially   87
everywhere in the world   189
example → good example would be having a mobile phone., A
excellent   14
excited by [at] ~ , be   155
exhibit   22-23
existing   95-96
expand   169
express → can't find any words to express
extremely   14

F

factor   168-69
feel close (closer) to ~   155
feel for ~   165
feel free to ~   → Please feel free to

drop in anytime.
feel good in our hands　52
feet　→ be rushed off my feet
find　→ I've found; we haven't found ~
fix up　144-45
following, for the　51, 53
following, the　59-60
follows　59-60
food　8
foot traffic　182-83
for details　52-53
for free　190
for getting to　58, 60-61
for the longest time　144-45
for the time being　151
forthwith　101-102
forward　→ look forward to finally meeting you
free　→ for free
from ~ points of view　188
~ from these three perspectives　189
fruit　7
fun　202
function　171-72
furthermore　5

G

get soaked　→ soaked
getting to　→ for getting to
get you　134
give (giving)　→ be giving
give command to ~　93
give up　149
globally　189
go camping　148
good example would be having a mobile phone., A　216
good idea　→ I would say it's a good idea to use ~
good time　→ it should be a good time
graduate from ~　105
graduate with honors　109-110
grateful for ~ , be　154-55

gratitude　→ as a gratitude of ~
grow up　132

H

hand　→ feel good in our hands; without putting our hands in our pockets
Happy New Year　85
hard-pressed　205-206
hard to imagine　128-29
have a nice feel　51-52
have been　18
have problem -ing　45
have problem with ~　45
hesitate　→ don't hesitate to ~
high demand　→ in high demand
hot　14
how about going to ~ ?　214
Human Resources　98, 100

I

I believe it's the right thing to do.　216
I'd like to describe why ~　188
if desired　115-16
if you need ~　163
If you're interested　142
If you would like to come　142
imagine　→ hard to imagine
Imagine a world without books.　216
I'm all set.　45
I'm looking forward to seeing you.　70
important　14
impossible　14
I'm sure the rest will be good　163
I'm sure the rest will help　163
I'm writing to you to complain about ~　77
in advance　33, 36
inconvenience　→ those inconvenienced
increase　169
indistinguishable　89-90
influx　182-83

inform A of [about] ~   61
information   → any information
ingenious   205, 207
in high demand   48
in pain   165
in person   37-38
instantaneously   193-94
Internet   → using the Internet
in time   158-59
involved with ~   118, 120
isolate   80-81
it ~ for ~ to ~   11
it is expected that S V   191
it'll be on me.   214
it should be a good time   214
it would be greatly appreciated   30-31
Il've found   148
I would like to know when it will arrive.   212
I would really appreciate it if ~   31
I would say it's a good idea to use public transportation.   216

J

join   → Would you care to join us?
Just bring yourself.   214
just right   55-56

K

kind [kindest] regards, (with)   20

L

leak   169
little, a   → a little
local patrol (group)   199, 202
long   → We are wondering how long it will take.
longest time   → for the longest time
look forward to finally meeting you   36
looking forward to seeing you   → I'm looking forward to seeing you.
Lots of love   135-36
luxurious   25, 27

M

management   72-73
merrier   → The more the merrier.
molestation   199, 202
moment   → at the moment
moreover   5
much trouble   78
my schedule is open   35

N

need   → if you need ~
need(s)   64-65
neither A nor B   10
nerve center   205-207
next to nothing   193-95
nice   27
nice feel   → have a nice feel
not all that   215
not A or B   11
not only A but (also) B   8-9, 87

O

off   → be off to ~
offering   → we are offering
office   → at your office
on   19
on and on   191
on a trial basis   30-31
one of those   158-59
on the other hand, ~   216
other   52-53
out for a drink after [afterwards]   68-69
overall   30-31

P

PA (system)   64-65
pain   → in pain
perspective   →~ from these three perspectives
place an order for ~   53
place on   113
pleasant to hold, be   52
Please feel free to drop in anytime.   214
pocket   → without putting our hands in our pockets
point   → from ~ points of view ; ~ using these three points as headings
point(s)   191
position of   19
possible   → Would it be possible to get a better discount?
problem   45, 200 ; → have problem -ing; have problem with ~
progress   168-69
prompt   81-82
put up with ~   176, 179

Q

qualifications   105, 107
quickly   43, 45

R

raise   168-69
regarding   98
regards   20
relate to   120
rest   → I'm sure the rest will be good; I'm sure the rest will help
reward(their efforts have recently been rewarded)   86
rich   14
right thing   → I believe it's the right thing to do.
rise   169
run-down   → become run-down

rush back   165-66
rush off   → be rushed off my feet

S

same   88
same as, the   88
schedule   → my schedule is open
score   191
score point   191
search for   27
self motivated, self-motivated   109-110
sensitive   93
set   → I'm all set.
sincerely yours   20
slightly   14
smooth   27
soaked (,be / get)   45
solely   48
sometime ~   35
so much trouble   78
soothing   27
sorry   → we are sorry ~
spare   37-38
stand   179
stay at ~   141
S tell (O) a story about ~   156
S tell O that ~   156
suburbs   176-77
sustain   47-48

T

take place   190
tastes   51-52
terrified   14
Thank you for your cooperation.   100
that   78-79
That being said, ~   216
The more the merrier.   214
then   8
therefore   5
things   176, 178
this is unacceptable   76, 78

this time 68
those inconvenienced 101-102
throughout the world 189
through to ～ 39-40
time → for the longest time; for the time being; in time; this time
time to ～ 95-96
token → as a token of ～
too 4-5
totally 14
touch ～ to 113
touch ～ with 113
trial basis → on a trial basis
trouble → so much trouble
truly honored 72-73
twiddle one's thumbs 205-206

U

unable to ～ 122
unacceptable → this is unacceptable
unforeseen 48-49
up for ～ 215
urge 44
using the Internet 188
～ using these three points as headings 189
utterly 14

V

very 14
view → from ～ points of view
vital 205-207

W

warm [warmest] regards, (with) 20
we are displeased with the actions of ～ 77
we are offering 93
we are sorry ～ 99
with warm [warmest] regards → warm [warmest] regards, (with)
with kind [kindest] regards → kind [kindest] regards, (with)
We are wondering how long it will take. 212
wear well 55-56
we have a complaint with ～ 77
we haven't found ～ 27
which 78-79
who 78-79
Why don't you go ～? 214
will 5-6
-wise 205-206
Wishing you a Happy New Year 85
without doubt 193-94
without putting our hands in our pockets 193-94
word → can't find any words to express
work from home 106
work on 19
world → everywhere in the world; throughout the world
worldwide 189
Would it be possible to get a better discount? 212
Would you care to join us? 214
Would you like to come with me? 214

Y

year-end party 69
yet 5
you have no idea 128-29
you must be ～ 161-62
yours 20
yours sincerely 20, 76, 79

英語便
www.eigobin.com

　英語便は、元々「コミュニケーションの必要性のなかで語学力を身に付けるための学習エンジン」としてスタートした。2005年5月に、「ソフトウェア開発技術のインターネット英語学習サービスへの適用による事業化」として東京都の経営革新法に認定され、東京都から融資を受け、同年6月にサイトの運営を開始した。初年度は400名の日本人英語学習者（無料モニター）に実際にウェブ上でコミュニケーションを試みてもらい、そこで得られた貴重な意見を踏まえて、コンテンツや添削システムの開発を進めた。そして同年9月、消費者ターゲットのインターネット商用サービスをスタートした。

　サービス開始直後から、信用できるネイティブ講師の英語添削が手頃な値段で受けられることが評判になり、おもに中上級の英語学習者を中心に、毎年会員数を増やしている。年齢幅は小学生（帰国子女のみ）から80代と幅広い。2016年1月現在、累計メンバー数は4万人以上、継続メンバー数は4500人以上である。

　講師は、アメリカ、イギリス、カナダ、オーストラリア、ニュージーランドほかの出身で、第一言語を英語とする者が務めている。ジャーナリスト、ライター、コピーライター、大学教師、さらには大手企業でビジネス英語コースを担当する講師など、各方面の英語のプロフェッショナルをそろえている。

　基本的にネイティブスピーカーが添削指導を担当するが、初級者は日本人スタッフのフォローや問い合わせを受けられる。

　6ヶ月単位のメンバー登録制になっており、メンバーは期間中、毎月2回の課題やTOEFL iBT, 英検1級、TOEIC SWテストの実践問題のほか、自分が書いたメールや日記、エッセイなどの添削指導も受けられる。

　また、メンバー同士のメールのやり取りや、掲示板での意見交換もできる（すべて英語）。

　学習目的で利用するだけでなく、実際に取引先に提出しなければならない英文のビジネス文書やメールの添削サービスを依頼するメンバーも少なくない。

　「お手頃な値段でネイティブ添削を提供する」こともサービス・ミッションの1つとしており、6ヶ月で1万9800円のコースから用意している（2016年1月現在）

　英語便は2015年で10年目を迎えた。今後も新しいサービスを打ち出し、日本人の英語学習をサポートしつづけたい。

＜英語便講師紹介＞

マーセル・モーリン（Marcel Morin）

（カナダ出身）
ビクトリア大学卒業。国内の大手企業で、ビジネス英語コース、TOEICのクラスを17年以上担当するほか、国内の英会話スクールでも主任講師として英会話指導にあたった。英語便では、コンテンツ監修とQ&A、ビジネス添削、メール添削を中心に担当している。

ポール・テヴリース（Paul de Vries）

（オーストラリア出身）
キャンベラ大学卒業。国内の英字新聞でのライター活動のほか、英語講師から英語教材のランゲージコンサルタントまで、幅広く活躍。英検二次試験の面接委員も務める。英語便では、おもにアカデミック添削、ビジネス添削を中心に担当している。

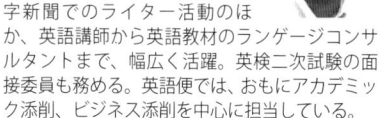

フランク・スピグニース（Frank Spignese）

（アメリカ出身）
エマーソン大学卒業。国内の英字新聞で音楽評論を執筆しながら、大学でも非常勤講師として英語を教える。英語便では、英文出版、翻訳チェックをはじめ、メールや日記を含め、幅広く添削指導している。

レイ・ノーリー（Leigh Norrie）

（イギリス出身）
グロスターシャー大学卒業。RSA/Cambridge certified 取得。国内の大学で非常勤講師として英語を教える一方、ライターとしても活躍する。英語便では、コンテンツ監修のほか、創作、学術論文を中心に、メールや日記の添削も担当している。

シャノン・ノダ（Shannon Noda）

（アメリカ出身）
セントマイケルズ大学卒業。国内の高校・中学で10年以上英語教師を務め、教材の開発やESSクラブのコーチを含む英語教育全般に携わっている。また、英検、TOEFLのライティングを教える経験が長く、英語便ではアカデミック添削を中心に担当している。

キャメロン・タン（Cameron Tan）

（オーストラリア出身）
ニューサウスウエールズ大学卒業。国内の英語学校で講師を務めたあと、現在はシドニーでコピーライターとして活動している。英語便では、創作、メール、日記から、アカデミックなものまで幅広く添削指導する。

ルーカス・ジャック＝サドゥニヤッキ（Lucas Jack-Sadiwnyki）

（カナダ出身）
トレント大学卒業/TEFL・TESOL取得。国内の英語学校で英会話講師を務め、カリキュラムやテキスト作成も担当していた。英語便では、メール、日記、エッセイ全般の添削を担当している。

テレース・ピッカースギル（Therese Pickersgill）

（カナダ出身）
国内の英語学校で英会話講師として、キッズからシニアのクラスまで、幅広く教えていた。英語便では、メール、日記、エッセイ全般の添削を担当している。

※英語便には、ほかにもネイティブ添削スタッフが常駐しています。

ネイティブ添削で学ぶ英文ライティング
REAL ENGLISH WRITING THROUGH CORRECTIONS

● 2012 年 2 月 14 日　初版発行 ●
● 2016 年 2 月 26 日　4 刷発行 ●

●著者●
英語便

Copyright © 2012 by Eigobin

発行者　●　関戸雅男
発行所　●　株式会社　研究社
〒 102-8152　東京都千代田区富士見 2-11-3
電話　営業 03-3288-7777（代）　編集 03-3288-7711（代）
振替　00150-9-26710
http://www.kenkyusha.co.jp/

イラスト　●　吉野浩司
装丁　●　久保和正
組版・レイアウト　●　mute beat
編集協力　●　増子久美・高見沢紀子
印刷所　●　研究社印刷株式会社
ISBN 978-4-327-45244-5 C1082　Printed in Japan

価格はカバーに表示してあります。
本書の無断複写（コピー）は著作権法上での例外を除き、禁じられています。
落丁本、乱丁本はお取り替え致します。
ただし、古書店で購入したものについてはお取り替えできません。